DARLING,
PLEASE

don't forget to

BRING BACK

THIS BOOK

ex libris

Let's Bring Back:

THE LOST LANGUAGE EDITION

Library of Congress Cataloging-in-Publication Data.

Blume, Lesley M. M.

Let's bring back : the lost language edition : a collection of forgotten-yet-delightful words, phrases,
praises, insults, idioms, and literary flourishes from eras past / Lesley M. M. Blume.

p. cm.

ISBN 978-1-4521-0530-7

1. English language--Etymology. 2. English language--Terms and phrases. 3. Popular culture. I. Title.
II. Title: Let us bring back. III. Title: Lost language edition. IV. Title: Collection of forgotten-yet-
delightful words, phrases, praises, insults, idioms, and literary flourishes from eras past.

PE1574.B623 2012   .

422--dc23

2012026449

Manufactured in China

DESIGNED BY TRACY SUNRIZE JOHNSON

ILLUSTRATIONS BY MARY KATE McDEVITT

10 9 8 7 6 5 4 3 2

Chronicle Books LLC
680 Second Street
San Francisco, California 94107

WWW.CHRONICLEBOOKS.COM

LET'S
BRING BACK:

••• THE LOST LANGUAGE EDITION •••

A Collection of

FORGOTTEN-YET-DELIGHTFUL

WORDS, PHRASES, PRAISES, INSULTS, IDIOMS,

and

Literary Flourishes

FROM ERAS PAST

Lesley M. M. Blume

CHRONICLE BOOKS
SAN FRANCISCO

AS WE ALL KNOW, NOTHING FALLS OUT OF FASHION LIKE FASHION. History has relegated thousands of adornments to the ash bin, from togas to bustles to turbans. Yet, somehow these "glad rags" always manage to stage comebacks, sneaking into our modern wardrobes in various guises. Once-fashionable words, on the other hand, have far less comeback savvy. Once a word or phrase is regarded as passé, it usually stays on the "Don't" list forever, with little hope for redemption. It seems dreadfully unfair, but as our grandparents used to say, "That's just the way the cookie crumbles."

Over the decades, centuries, and millennia, thousands of entertaining, poignant, mischievous, and brilliant expressions have been birthed by cultural vogues and just as quickly fallen victim to them as well. Some of the rejects are far more nuanced and descriptive than the modern words and idioms conjured up to take their places—and in many cases, no satisfying substitute has been offered up at all.

Clearly, then, we must take action. Introducing *Let's Bring Back: The Lost Language Edition*, whose mission is to revive and preserve hundreds of perfectly delightful words, phrases, idioms, and other literary flourishes from bygone eras. The restoration of these terms is not merely a quirky, history-minded pastime; rather, it's a necessary act of intervention to help us disadvantaged modern creatures express ourselves cleverly and with flair once again.

Some of the featured words have been obsolete for hundreds of years; others were discarded as recently as the 1990s, but are still as revival-worthy as their ancient counterparts. Many of the following expressions aren't fully extinct, but can be considered an endangered species of charming, grandmotherly sayings (and don't forget that grandmothers—while they may *look* sweet and nonjudgmental— often have sharper tongues than anyone else in the room). The words and phrases in all of these categories have been included in the book as a plea for their ongoing use by future generations.

An important caveat: *Let's Bring Back: The Lost Language Edition* is certainly not meant to be an all-inclusive dictionary of historical slang. There are many such tomes available, some of which are several thousand pages thick and heavy as cement blocks; consult one of these fine catalogues for an exhaustive etymological history. Consult this book, on the other hand, for a curated list of outmoded-yet-splendid slang words that are still relevant—and often highly amusing—when dropped into conversation or correspondence today.

The following pages celebrate a sampling of terms selected through a years-long literary scavenger hunt. Among the countless sources culled: Old Hollywood "pictures," children's storybooks, nineteenth-century "muckraking" newspaper articles, beatnik play scripts, the Bible, and chirpy mid-century frozen food advertisements. The wise-cracking Jean Harlow in the 1933 film *Bombshell* was as juicy a source of colorful vintage vocabulary as the comedies and tragedies of William Shakespeare. Some of the included phrases are as old (and lusty) as Cleopatra; many of them are rooted in our agrarian past. Although most of us today may be far removed from the daily routines of earth-tilling and chicken-farming, we can still appreciate the inherent wisdom and applicability of these old-world countryside sayings.

TEXT CONTINUES NEXT PAGE ⟫→

Thumbing through historical slang and idiom dictionaries, it is astonishing to see how many thousands of centuries-old expressions are still in regular use today. *Let's Bring Back: The Lost Language Edition* concentrates on lost or now-underused words, but research for this book showed that other lucky words—for whatever reason—have enjoyed remarkable staying power. As we casually utter these phrases, we often know nothing about their inception and evolution; we have no concept of how they made their way into our personal vocabularies in the first place. Who can remember the first time they were instructed not to "cry over spilled milk" or told about "the school of hard knocks"? These phrases just seem to have always surrounded us as naturally as the air we breathe. But they were taught to our parents by their parents and so on down the line, sometimes as far back as a dozen generations, and often boast surprising origins.

It's also fascinating to discover how many different meanings a single word can accrue over the years. For example, most of us likely associate the word "groovy" with 1960s flower children and hippies; but had you hollered out the word a century earlier, your contemporaries would have thought that you were talking about a sardine. While we're on the subject of marine life, consider the word "oyster." To us, it signifies a mollusk and a culinary delicacy; yet in the 1800s, an oyster was also "a jolly good guy." Before *that*, however, it meant a gob of phlegm. Some phrases are so relentlessly indecisive that their various definitions or connotations entirely contradict each other: "up a gum tree," for example, can either mean "trapped in a dangerous situation" or "out of danger's reach," depending on the context (not to mention the attitude of the person uttering the expression).

From a certain point of view, however, in the world of words, the more things change, the more they stay the same. Perusing the vocabularies of generations past, you realize that the same types of people and situations existed in ancient Rome or Elizabethan England that surface in contemporary New York City or Los Angeles—or Beaver Creek, Montana, for that matter. Human vocabulary may have changed, but human behavior has not. People "got out of the wrong side of the bed" in Caesar's day; the world has always been riddled with "knaves," "seek-sorrows," "gadabouts," "whipsters," and "dandiprats." Amorous couples have "firkytoodled" for years, and "ribs" (wives) have given "curtain lectures" (chastisements issued to world-weary husbands at bedtime) for millennia. Revisiting the vernaculars of bygone eras—even the forgotten parts of those vernaculars—can provide a sense of continuity, even camaraderie, with our ancestors, whom we resemble in so many ways.

So, without further ado, let's settle in and rediscover some wonderful words from the past. From "mollycoddles" to "rapscallion," from "batty-fanging" to "tippybobs," from "attic salt" to "ziff," there are many pleasing old expressions ready to be whispered, shouted, hissed, purred, sputtered, and exclaimed once again.

A BIRD IN THE HAND IS WORTH TWO IN THE BUSH

Meaning that it's better to be content with what you have than to risk losing everything in pursuit of a bigger opportunity. One source says that this proverb has its roots in medieval falconry, where a bird (i.e., a falcon) in the hand was a valuable asset, "and certainly worth more than two in the bush (the prey)."

A DIME A DOZEN

I.e., cheap and/or common; easy to come by. The phrase may refer to a package deal offered by merchants for penny candy in the early twentieth century: if you bought in bulk (a dozen), you'd get twelve pieces of candy for the price of ten. ("Those plaid Burberry scarves are a dime a dozen these days.")

ABOVE MY BEND

Beyond one's power: "I don't know why she wears that ghastly wig every day, but it's above my bend to do anything about it."

ACE OF SPADES

An old term for "widow."

ACQUAINTANCE

Today the word "friend" is used rather carelessly; it should be reserved for the most hallowed of relationships. One rarely hears the word "acquaintance" anymore—a polite, cunning catchall term that strikes the perfect balance between affiliation and distance.

ADMIRAL OF THE RED

Apparently this old British phrase indicated a person whose red face belied a love of liquor.

AFTER-CLAP

When something unexpected—and unpleasant—happens after a matter was thought to be resolved—like an unpleasant, sharp rumble of thunder after the storm has passed.

AFTERNOON FARMER

One who wastes a great opportunity. Farmers have long been notorious early-risers, tilling the earth and feeding chickens and so on; those who laze about in bed are most certainly rewarded with sullen crops and ornery livestock.

AGREE LIKE PICKPOCKETS IN A FAIR

I.e., not to agree at all—often purposefully. Any observer of the workings of the American Congress these days should be familiar with this term. Another good, old-fashioned variation: "Agree like cats and dogs."

ALL HAT AND NO CATTLE

A withering old Texan term for a blusterer, someone who boasts about himself without any evidence of the professed accomplishments. ("He claims to be quite the ladies' man, but he's all hat and no cattle.") Another splendid animal-world variation: "All his geese are swans," meaning that the person in question always exaggerates.

ALL MY EYE

An incredulous response to a story, likely invoked over countless bridge games in the past.

SEE ALSO "'WELL, I NEVER': AMUSINGLY QUAINT REACTION PHRASES," (PAGE 211)

ALL THE GO

Fashionable. ("Isn't it odd how hats with big animal ears are all the go this season?")

ALL THE TEA IN CHINA

A late nineteenth-century phrase meaning "not for any price." China was—and remains—one of the world's leading exporters of tea, so "all the tea in China" must amount to a pretty considerable pile. ("You couldn't drag me to her dreary bridal shower for all the tea in China.")

fig. 1: ONE IN A MILLION

ALL-OVERISH

Feeling not exactly well, yet not exactly sick—something along the lines of a preamble to illness. We have no contemporary word that describes this sensation as aptly.

ALSO-RAN

A phrase that emerged in the 1890s, indicating a horse that loses races. It was also used as an insidiously devastating term for an unsuccessful contender. ("You don't need to worry about any competition from *that* also-ran of an author; his book is a total bore.")

HE'S QUITE AN ADONIS

Historical Figures and Characters Who Became Archetypes

All of the archetypes listed below have been around for quite some time, but as the source material from which they sprang ages, chances increase that these archetypes will fall out of fashion. Let's keep them around; we all know people who meet the following descriptions.

....

Adonis

As a noun, "Adonis" means an extremely handsome young man. Adonis the person (or personage, rather) was a Greek mythological figure, a human so ridiculously gorgeous that he inspired a feud between smitten goddesses Aphrodite and Persephone. It's a long story, but eventually he was killed by a wild boar for his troubles; scholars still dispute which jealous god unleashed the pig on the youth. Whoever was responsible, at least Adonis got to die in Aphrodite's arms.

Jekyll and Hyde

The dictionary definition of a "Jekyll and Hyde" is a person "marked by dual personality, one aspect of which is good and the other bad." The term hails from Robert Louis Stevenson's *The Strange Case of Dr. Jekyll and Mr. Hyde* (1886); you could visit with the novel's protagonist, Dr. Jekyll, one evening and encounter a perfectly pleasant gentleman, but the next night, he might very well be out on the town as Mr. Hyde, "batty-fanging" (see page 18) young maidens and elder statesmen.

Jezebel

Another biblical offering, Jezebel the person was a vicious queen
(the wife of Ahab, king of Israel) who conspired to have the
prophets of Israel destroyed. As a noun, Jezebel (often rendered
in lowercase form) means "a wicked, shameless woman."

Judas

This term usually describes "a person treacherous enough to
betray a friend; a traitor." It is also defined as "an animal decoy
used to lead other animals to their slaughter." The biblical figure
who gave his name to this term is Judas Iscariot, the apostle who
betrayed Jesus to his enemies for thirty lousy pieces of silver.

Mrs. Grundy

Poor Mrs. Grundy; she sounds so very unpleasant. As both
a noun and a fictional character in the play *Speed the Plough*
(1798) by Thomas Morton, she epitomizes a "narrow-minded,
conventional person who is extremely critical of any breach
of propriety."

Pollyanna

This old-fashioned term refers to "a person who is constantly or
excessively optimistic," inspired by the title character in a best-
selling 1913 novel by Eleanor Porter. In this book, Pollyanna's
philosophy of life centers on what she chirpily calls "The Glad
Game," which consists of finding something to be glad about in
every situation, no matter how dire. For example, when stashed
in an attic by a dour aunt, Pollyanna delights in the view from
her perch. *Nothing* gets this dame down—not even a car accident
that breaks both of her legs. (Ol' Pollyanna's take on that situation: Well, I'm glad that I *had* legs that worked, at least.)

ANGEL'S OIL

A bribe. An "angel" was a fifteenth-century gold coin.

ANKLE-BITER

An amusing term for "child" (presumably a rambunctious, toothy one), popularized in the mid-1800s. Children's book author Roald Dahl—famous for creating archetypical brats in his novels—likely would have adored this phrase.

SEE ALSO "CHATTERBOX"

ANYTHINGARIAN

"An indifferentist, a Jack-of-both-sides," as colorfully stated by *The Dictionary of Slang and Colloquial English* (1905). The "anythingarian" might actually be a distant cousin to the pragmatist.

ARRIVISTE

A wonderfully nasty yet erudite term for "social climber." The good news: most social climbers won't know the word and might think that you're actually paying them a compliment, because "arriviste" simply sounds so glamorous.

AS I LIVE AND BREATHE

Another splendid old-fashioned exclamation. Its primness would prove particularly funny if uttered in reaction to raunchy news.

ATTIC SALT

An offering from the 1700s, "attic salt" was another term for "wit." Various definitions qualify the variety of wit as being either "dry, delicate wit," "biting wit," or "graceful, piercing wit." In any case, it referred to verbal salt produced in one's attic, or head. ("Dorothy Parker had enough attic salt to bore through an icy interstate highway.")

BAD APPLE

I.e., a nasty piece of work; someone filled with ill will. "Bad apples," "bad eggs," and "bad pennies" were also presumed to be corrupting creatures, as evidenced by the popular old saying "One bad apple spoils the barrel."

BALONEY

In addition to being a perfectly repulsive sort of deli meat, "baloney" was for years a popular synonym for "nonsense." In this context, baloney was usually issued in verbal bulk: "He *claims* that he's a descendant of George Washington, but that's a big bunch of baloney."

SEE ALSO "'HOGWASH AND HOOEY': CHARMING ARCANE WORDS FOR 'NONSENSE,'" (PAGE 94)

BARK UP THE WRONG TREE

To follow the wrong or mistaken course of action. This phrase began to surface in the early 1800s, and alludes to a dog barking up a tree while its prey nestles safely in the branches of another tree. Some sources attribute the phrase's origin to James Kirke Paulding's 1832 book *Westward Ho!*, which features the following passage:

> I begun to smoke him for one of those fellows that drive a sort of a trade of making books about old Kentuck and the western country: so I thought I'd set him barking up the wrong tree a little, and I told him some stories that were enough to set the Mississippi a-fire; but he put them all down in his book.

BARNACLES

An entertaining old synonym for "glasses." Barnacles were presumably only donned by people with mole-grade eyesight and nerdily reclusive tendencies.

fig. 2: A BIT TIGHT ON THE BRIDGE

BASTE

A *very* pleasing old word. To give someone a "good basting" meant to "thrash him soundly." Especially satisfying and victorious-sounding because it brings up images of basting a trussed and cooked turkey.

SEE ALSO "TURKEY"

BATTY-FANGING

This term—which means "a thorough beating"—*must* be revived immediately. It can be used as a verb ("I'll batty-fang the sass right out of that man") or a noun: "I'd love to give that whippersnapper a good batty-fanging."

BEAT ONE'S GUMS

A distinctly distasteful 1920s phrase for "idle chatter." Clearly it should be resurrected as a description for loud cellphone-talkers: "She stood next to me, gripping her iPhone and beating her gums for twenty solid minutes about her boring date the night before."

BECOMING

As in: "That color is very becoming on you," or "Rehab clearly becomes you."

BEE IN ONE'S BONNET

A preoccupation or obsession with a particular idea, one that buzzes around and around in your mind. The source of the phrase is unclear; some say that it's from Scotland, where men and boys sported "bonnets" in bygone eras; others assert that it simply refers to the protective headgear worn by beekeepers. Regardless, people have been getting "bees in their bonnets" for at least three centuries.

THE BEE'S KNEES

Animal Kingdom—Inspired Accolades from the 1920s

Saying "thank you" is such a trite way of expressing gratitude.
Instead, tell a deserving someone that he or she is "the bee's knees"—
i.e., "absolutely the best." The 1920s offered up all sorts of these
delightfully inane animal kingdom compliments, including:

The cat's meow

The cat's pajamas

The cat's whiskers

The duck's quack

The eel's ankle

The elephant's instep

The gnat's whistle

The oyster's earrings

The sardine's whiskers

The snake's hips

The tiger's spots

BEETLE-CRUSHER

A large, flat foot. The term should clearly be put into use again by shoe salespeople, who can use it while snickering about all of Cinderella's sisters trying on their delicate wares. ("Did you see her try to shovel her beetle-crusher into that Louboutin? Fat chance!")

SEE ALSO "STAMPERS"

BEGGARS CAN'T BE CHOOSERS

A cutting idiom best explained by the *American Heritage New Dictionary of Cultural Literacy*: "People who depend on the generosity of others are in no position to dictate what others give them." Once again, the exact origin is unclear, but it was used in a rather biting mid-1500s proverb by John Heywood:

> Beggers should be no choosers, but yet they will:
> Who can bryng a begger from choyse to begge still?

BEGGING the QUESTION

I'd like to bring back a useful expression from the science of logic, which has in the past few decades been misused so widely that it is now mostly employed to mean something else, leaving critics with no simple way to say what is wrong with a certain type of fallacious argument. The expression is "begging the question," which for many centuries meant one clear and simple thing: reasoning in a circle—that is, assuming the truth of that which you seek to prove. Nowadays, most people say "P begs the question Q" when they mean merely "P raises the question Q." This makes our language poorer.

ANTHONY GOTTLIEB • AUTHOR OF *THE DREAM OF REASON*; FORMER EXECUTIVE EDITOR OF *THE ECONOMIST*

BELLYACHE

To complain. A perfectly apt old term,
as no one likes a complainer *or* a bellyache.

BEND SOMEONE'S EAR

To talk at someone without interruption; in other words; to drone on and on and on, inducing near-suicidal boredom in the unfortunate listener. We all know an ear-bender; this phrase must be revived.

BENT OUT OF SHAPE

Angry about something. Historically, people usually referred to someone's *nose* being bent out of shape, which sounds, of course, quite painful and understandably upsetting. A similarly colorful utterance appears in the 1961 film *Breakfast at Tiffany's*, in which Hollywood agent O. J. Berman agitates writer Paul Varjack, and then implores: "Don't get yourself *all tense and sore*, pal—it's a party."

THE BERRIES

A quaint, sweet compliment: "That gal is the berries."

SEE ALSO "'THE BEE'S KNEES': ANIMAL KINGDOM-INSPIRED ACCOLADES FROM THE 1920S," (PAGE 19)

BET YOU DOLLARS TO DOG BISCUITS

An old phrase invoked when the bettor is extremely confident of a certain outcome: "I bet you dollars to dog biscuits that she'll be an hour late, as usual." However, the modern variation—"dollars to doughnuts"—is equally amusing, albeit more fattening.

BETTER THAN A POKE IN THE EYE WITH A SHARP STICK

A resigned, old-fashioned response to hearing about a mediocre outcome. Were you expecting roses on your anniversary, and got carnations instead? Console yourself that the booby prize remains "better than a poke in the eye with a sharp stick."

BEZONIAN

Dating back to the late 1500s, "bezonian" is an archaic term for a rascal. And not just any old rascal, mind you, but an "*indigent* rascal."

BIDDY

The popularly cited synonym for this three-hundred-year-old word is equally delightful: "fussbudget." The fussbudget in question was usually a fussy old woman—often of the gossipy and interfering variety.

SEE ALSO "GADABOUT"

BIRDS AND THE BEES

An innocent-sounding euphemism for "sex." Nervous parents explaining the facts of life to Junior and Junior Miss often invoked the birds and the bees—and sometimes got some surprising results:

> What a kid I got. I told him about the birds and the bees, and he told me about the butcher and my wife.

—Rodney Dangerfield, comedian

BIT-OF-STUFF

A divine phrase for a peacocky, overdressed man: a bit-of-stuff strutting his stuff.

BITCHFOXLY

A woman of the night. The word memorably turns up in *1776*, historian David McCullough's seminal book about the birth year of the American Revolution, as he describes the lascivious behavior of the Continental Army during its brief tenure in New York City. According to one witness, the "bitchfoxly, jades, hags, [and] strums" conducted "their employ which has become very lucrative."

BLASTED

Accursed. ("That blasted pen just exploded in my pants pocket and leaked ink all over my crotch.")

BLINKERS

Another divine old synonym for "eyeglasses."

SEE ALSO "BARNACLES," "CHEATERS," "PEEPERS," *and* "SPECTACLES"

BLOOD FROM A TURNIP

A slightly more idiosyncratic version of the old saying "You can't get blood from a stone" (i.e., you can't extract what isn't there to begin with). When you think about it, the variations on this theme are arguably endless: "You can't get blood from a corn cob" . . . "You can't get blood from a Tic Tac" . . . and so on.

BLOW A FUSE

To get extremely surly or fly into a rage. ("Mom really blew her fuse when the dog snatched the Thanksgiving turkey off the counter.") Another variation: "blow one's jets."

fig. 3: I SAID "MAIN MENU"!!!

BLOW SMOKE

Someone who "blows smoke" is making exaggerated claims or lying. In quainter times, the liar in question was often said to be "blowing smoke up someone's sleeve"—or under cruder circumstances, into intimate parts of the listener's anatomy.

BLOW THE WORKS

To confess or spill the beans.

BLOW TOWN

To get out of town, usually after a nasty or illegal "kerfuffle" (see page 109). An amusing cousin to this phrase: "let's blow this popsicle stand," meaning "let's get out of this boring place." One imagines the utterer of these mid-century phrases to be wearing a white undershirt with a box of cigarettes rolled up in his sleeve, hair greased and carefully combed into an Elvis-like pompadour.

BLUENOSE

A prudish, puritanical person.

fig. 4: DINNER WITH THE SWELLS

BON TON

A rather old-fashioned term meaning "fashionable society," most frequently used in sentences such as: "These days, she's been swanning about with the *bon ton*, with hardly a thought for her old friends and acquaintances."

BOOBY-HATCH

A crazy house. An equally pleasing synonym: a "loony bin." Usually used sardonically when describing a domestic or professional setting: "What a booby-hatch I live in—everyone in my family is nuts."

SEE ALSO "'CRAZY FOR YOU': OLD-FASHIONED LABELS FOR THE MENTALLY UNSOUND," (PAGE 43)

BORN YESTERDAY

A term for "naïve." Often screeched out by silver screen tarts and broads in Old Hollywood: "Whaddya think—that I was born yestahday?"

BORROW TROUBLE

One definition of this expression asserts that it means "to do something that is unnecessary and may cause future harm or inconvenience." Yet it was also used when someone was fussing unnecessarily.

BOSH

First popular in the mid-1800s, this word means "absurd or foolish talk."

BOTHERATION

An exclamation of frustration: "Botheration! Someone ate all of my Cocoa Puffs!" Good alternatives: "Confound it!" or "Deuce take it!"

BOUNDER

An obtrusive, ill-bred man; a cad.

BOUQUETS TO YOU

I.e., "congratulations"—best used in a sarcastic manner from a jealous competitor. "You got first prize in the beauty pageant *again*? Well, bouquets to you."

BOWSERBAG

A jaunty alternate name for the plain old doggy bag.

BOX SOMEONE'S EARS

To give someone a punishing smack. In the old days, the phrase was often incorporated in nannyish reproaches: "William, if you don't clean up your room, I'll box your ears."

BOZO

A whole list of unpleasant adjectives attach themselves to this early twentieth-century word (which predates the once-popular television character "Bozo the Clown"); it describes a man who is "big," "stupid," "rude," "obnoxious," or "annoying"—and perhaps even all of the above at once.

BRAT

Underused in today's vernacular—which is odd, considering that brats appear to be more rife than ever. The ultimate brat poster girl: Veruca Salt in Roald Dahl's book *Charlie and the Chocolate Factory*, whose shenanigans in the 1971 film adaptation prompted the factory's resident Oompa Loompas to immortalize her with a song, in which they asked,

> *"Who do you blame when your kid is a brat?*
> *Pampered and spoiled like a Siamese cat."*

Their answer: Blaming the kids would be a "lie and a shame." Rather, contend the Oompa Loompas, blame rests squarely with "the mother and the father."

BRICK

A term conjured up in the 1800s to describe a good, reliable person. ("That old Mr. Peabody is a regular brick: always here to help in a pinch.")

BRIGHT AS A BUTTON

Quick-minded; clever. An old idiom usually used to describe children. ("She's bright as a button—unlike her mother, who's dull as dirt.")

BRING SOMEONE TO TIME

To reel someone in or teach him or her a lesson—usually applied as a remedy for braggarts and those habitually overstepping their bounds.

BUGBEAR

Any source—real or imagined—of needless fear or anxiety. The word goes back to the 1500s, when it signified a literal bear-demon with an appetite for young children. It was later used in lighter circumstances, as evidenced by this passage in renowned society hostess Elsa Maxwell's 1957 book, *How to Do It, or the Lively Art of Entertaining*:

> That old bugbear, money, is the most common defense I hear
> from women who are afraid to give parties simply because they
> can't afford to entertain on a gilt-edged scale.

BULLY FOR YOU

I.e., "Good for you." Hurrah. Yay. Congratulations. (As with "Bouquets to you" (see
page 26), likely best resurrected in sarcastic
situations.)

BULLYRAG

To scold mercilessly.

BUM

We all know what the noun "bum" means today, but it used to be used as an
adjective as well, to indicate something that was bad: "a bum check." Or as
Breakfast at Tiffany's heroine Holly Golightly states while smoking a Picayune
cigarette upon learning that her lover has jilted her: "Tastes bum . . . but divine."

fig. 5: BE PREPARED

BUMBERSHOOT

A circa 1895 word for "umbrella"—very Mary
Poppins-chic.

BUNCH-OF-FIVES

A fist. ("I'd like to repay that guy for all of his back-
talk with a bunch-of-fives.")

BUNK

Hogwash.

SEE ALSO "'HOGWASH AND HOOEY': CHARMING
ARCHAIC WORDS FOR 'NONSENSE,'" (PAGE 94)

BURR UNDER THE SADDLE

A source of irritation.

BUSTER

An old-fashioned form of address to a man or boy—often uttered in conjunction with an admonishment: "Watch where you put those hands, buster."

BUSY BEAVER

A terribly industrious person.

BUSYBODY

This funny old term—which means "a meddling snoop"—dates back five centuries. It remains especially apt because serious meddlers are indeed feverishly busy with their chosen occupation.

SEE ALSO "BIDDY" *and* "GADABOUT"

BUTTERFINGERS

A clumsy person; someone who frequently drops things, as though his or her fingers have been greased with butter. Modern Sagittarians—renowned as the klutziest members of the zodiac—should become reacquainted with this term.

BUY THE FARM

To die.

SEE ALSO "KICK THE BUCKET" *and* "JOIN THE MAJORITY"

CABBAGE

To pilfer; filch. ("Those mice cabbaged every scrap of cheese from the larder.") The origins of this use for the word are unclear, although one dictionary suggests that it may be "related to Old French *cabas* (theft)." It was also slang for money.

CAKE'S NOT WORTH THE CANDLE

I.e., the result isn't worth the effort you'd have to put in to achieve it. It could also imply a person who's gotten above her station, who's sporting luxurious new adornments that sit uneasily upon her.

CAKEWALK

An easily accomplished task. The word likely stemmed from the nineteenth-century cakewalk dance phenomenon, in which prancing couples would compete for a prize: those who strutted with the fanciest steps won a cake at the contest's conclusion. The performances could be elaborate, but were generally considered light recreation—and the phrase "takes the cake" also emerged from the ritual.

CAITIFF

A Middle English word for a low, base, despicable person. ("That caitiff said he was going to the bathroom, but then he snuck out of the restaurant and stuck me with the bill!")

CAPER

An underused word. Its primary definition, courtesy of Dictionary.com: "A prank, trick, or harebrained escapade." Secondary definition: "A frivolous, carefree episode or activity." Perhaps the word's comparative rareness can be seen as a societal commentary: we have too little time these days to indulge in "carefree activities" and therefore have less use for the words that describe them.

SEE ALSO "HIJINKS"

CARD

A witty, entertaining, and eccentric person.

CARE A FIG

Usually preceded by "I don't . . .", this old phrase was a prim alternative to "I don't give a damn." Another great variation: "Care a pin."

CARPET-KNIGHT

A ladies' man; a frequenter of drawing rooms; a creature devoted to languorous pleasure. It was also used as a disparaging term for a soldier who managed to avoid the battlefield, an idler.

CARRY CORN

To carry one's success well. The phrase was often used pejoratively: "He got that surprise promotion, but God knows he doesn't carry corn well."

CARRY ME OUT!

An old-fashioned exclamation uttered upon hearing news that seems too good to be true: "Our houseguests are leaving a few days early? Carry me out!"

CASH OR CHECK?

Meaning "Kiss me now . . . or later?" Used delightfully in the 1949 film *Adam's Rib*, in which the question was posited by actress Katharine Hepburn to her onscreen and real-life paramour Spencer Tracy.

CASTLES IN THE AIR

Utterly impractical ideas. Such a charming phrase that it makes the concoction of impractical ideas seem like an appealing pastime.

CATCH-AS-CATCH-CAN

According to one dictionary, this phrase emerged in the mid-1700s, and meant "using any available means or method" to achieve a certain end. A related, secondary definition: "without a specific plan or without order." ("The Boxcar Children lived a catch-as-catch-can existence, making a home out of an abandoned railway car and using broken dishes found at a nearby dump.")

CATCH FORTY WINKS

Catching said winks meant to embark on a brief but revitalizing nap. No one can agree on how the creator of the idiom decided upon *forty* winks, but assorted experts point out that in bygone eras, that number was considered quite lucky.

CAUGHT DEAD

As in, "I wouldn't be caught dead lunching with that woman in public." A famous use of the phrase took place in the 1957 film *Funny Face*, in which dictatorial fashion magazine editor Maggie Prescott has just waged an international campaign to make the color pink all the rage, urging "women everywhere" to buy pink bags, shoes, toothpaste, shampoo, kitchen sinks, and the like.

The campaign succeeds wildly, but one of her colleagues notices that Maggie is still sporting a blue-gray skirt suit. "I haven't seen a woman in two weeks in anything but pink," the colleague tells her. "What about you?" Looking appalled, Maggie replies: "Me? I wouldn't be caught dead."

CHANCE THE DUCKS

A nineteenth-century phrase meaning to forge ahead, come what may. ("It looks like rain, but let's chance the ducks and have the picnic anyway.")

CHATTERBOX

Someone who chatters on and on, constantly and obliviously. The eighteenth century also produced the delightful "chatter-basket," an old nursery term for a tirelessly verbose child.

CHEAPSKATE

A miserly, stingy person. Good, old-fashioned synonyms: "scrooge" and "skinflint."

CHEATERS

Eyeglasses. Another offering from the colorful vernacular of the 1920s.

fig. 6: ALL THE BETTER
TO SEE YOU WITH

SEE ALSO "BARNACLES," "PEEPERS," *and* "SPECTACLES"

CHEW THE FAT

To gab, 1800s-style. Also: "chew the rag."

CHICKABIDDY

A young girl. Perhaps a "biddy" with training wheels on (see page 22).

CHICKEN-HEARTED

Cowardly, as evidenced by the lyrics to "Chicken Hearted" by Roy Orbison, in which he declares himself "yellow," "scared at his own shadow," and moans repeatedly "I'm chicken-hearted."

CHISELER

A swindler or cheater. One memorable use of the word comes to us courtesy of *The Speakeasies of 1932* by Gordon Kahn and Al Hirschfeld, describing Bath Club on West 53rd Street: "[there are] flunkies in droves. Hat boys who won't touch a coat, and cloak boys beneath whose station it is to handle a Borsalino. There are chiselers, not recognizable at the first glance, but spottable after a while."

CHOPS

A Jazz Age term for "mouth"; it was also slang for technical virtuosity. Jazz icon Louis Armstrong famously rasped about his chops in "Tenderly":

> *You took my chops 'way from bops*
> *Tenderly*

CHUMP

A stupid person of the gullible variety.

SEE ALSO "BORN YESTERDAY"

CINCH

A cakewalk (see page 31).

CLACK-BOX

Meaning "a garrulous person," clack-box is slightly more derisive than "chatterbox" and even more fun to say.

CLAPTRAP

Stemming from 1730s stage vernacular, claptrap is officially defined as "high-sounding but empty language." More specifically, it means a linguistic "trick that was meant to catch applause" (i.e., trap claps), but lacked substance. Visit any one of a variety of political rallies today, and you'll see why this apt term needs to be resurrected.

CLASSY

Elegantly or admirably stylish; of a high caliber. This late nineteenth-century term implies that a "classy" person or object belongs to the realm of the upper classes, but the term opens itself to paradoxical ridicule: "She's got tons of class—lower class, that is."

CLEVER-CLOGS

An old British term for an annoying person who invariably has the right answer to everything, and purports to be smarter than everyone around him. Also: "clever Dick."

CLODHOPPER

A clumsy country-bumpkin type.

CLOSE BUT NO CIGAR

What you tell someone who's fallen *just* short of accomplishing his or her goal. In ye olde days, fairground game stalls gave out cigars as prizes; if you missed hitting the bottle off the stand with a baseball, even by a hair, you were close, but got no cigar for your efforts. The bottom line: history usually doesn't record or respect the memory of a near miss. It's either a win— or nothing.

CLOSE SHAVE

A more visceral predecessor to the phrase "close call." Anything that evokes a sharp blade passing over a vulnerable throat is bound to make the averted situation sound more urgent and frightening.

COCK-A-HOOP

Excited: "I couldn't be more cock-a-hoop for the hoedown at the barn tonight." Other definitions include "exuberantly boastful" or "awry."

COCKAMAMIE

Ridiculous and pointless: "Her head positively teems with cockamamie notions and schemes."

COLLYWOBBLES

Another word for "stomachache." One imagines that you'd feel better by simply saying the phrase "I've got the collywobbles"—which is more than enough reason to bring it back.

COLT'S TOOTH

An elderly person with a "colt's tooth" has unbecomingly juvenile tastes— *très* Humbert Humbert.

COME TO POINTS

To find oneself in a swordfight: "They came to points over that last sticky bun."

GOING POSTAL

Memorable Phrases from "Clueless"

At first glance, the 1995 cult film *Clueless* looks as superficial as a bright pink press-on fingernail. However, writer-director Amy Heckerling based this Los Angeles comedy about Cher Horowitz, a vacuous yet well-intentioned teenage fashionista, on Jane Austen's 1815 novel, *Emma*, and it was immediately embraced as a savvy satire of myopic, materialistic American culture. The script's updated valley girl language also rewrote teenage vernacular for more than a generation, helping to popularize '90s phrases such as "keeping it real," "as *if*," "the bomb," and "phat." (It also reintroduced a lot of divine Rat Pack–era terms, e.g., "doll," "fin," and "knock me a kiss.")

Some of the more memorable *Clueless* words and phrases:

Digits

A phone number.

Four-one-one

Background information on someone ("Here's the four-one-one on Mr. Hall"), from the bygone days when people regularly dialed "411" to get contact information from an operator.

Going postal

Losing it, going crazy. Refers to a rash of 1990s
shootings and other violent incidents that took place
in post offices across the country.

Give someone a toothache

When someone says that another person gives
him or her a toothache, it means the latter is incredibly
sweet. In other words, an expression for a crush.

Jeepin'

I.e., amorous activities in an automobile – or
"vehicular sex," as one of the film's characters puts it.

Loadies

Drugheads; people who are loaded all of the time.
("Sometimes they come to class and say bonehead
things, and we all laugh, of course.
But no respectable girl actually dates them.")

Monet

A person who only looks good *a la distance*.
("It's like a painting, see? From far away, it's okay,
but up close, it's a big old mess.")

COMFOOZLED

Exhausted; spent.

SEE ALSO "DUMB-FOOZLED"

COMRADE

It might not bring back the rosiest of memories for some — but considering that most of us feel like we work in some version of a Soviet-style bureaucracy, the word "comrade" is actually far more accurate than "colleague."

CONDIDDLE

This old-guard word just sounds so much more innocuous than its modern synonyms: "steal" or "pilfer." Therefore, it's likely to be revived by would-be thieves — or the attorneys who ultimately represent those thieves in court.

CONFLABBERATION

A hullaballoo.

COOKING WITH GAS

Meaning "now we're really moving along," or some approximation thereof. The phrase came originally from an old advertisement for gas stoves, which declared that gas is faster, easier, cleaner, and better than cooking with wood.

COOK ONE'S GOOSE

A nineteenth-century Americanism, cooking someone's goose means to ruin him, or at least drag him through the ringer (and back). There was often a lot of talk of "cooking one's own goose" too — which shows that the human tendency to be our own worst enemies is a time-honored tradition.

COOL CAT

I used the phrase "cool cat"—as in "He is one cool cat"—a few times back in 2008 to describe then-candidate Barack Obama. While I would hesitate to apply it to a(ny) sitting president of the United States, for fear of committing *lèse majesté*, it strikes me as a circa 1950's phrase that ought to be brought back into circulation. But whatever, man.

CHRISTOPHER BUCKLEY • POLITICAL SATIRIST; AUTHOR OF FOURTEEN BOOKS, INCLUDING *NO WAY TO TREAT A FIRST LADY*, *THANK YOU FOR SMOKING*, AND *THEY EAT PUPPIES, DON'T THEY?*

COOL ONE'S HEELS

To wait—or, rather, be forced to wait until you calm down from some kerfuffle. In the old days—as now—people often cooled their heels in jail. And thus riseth the slang word "cooler," a synonym for prison.

CORN IN EGYPT

This term denotes a large amount of money or a "plentiful supply" of some commodity. It comes to us courtesy of Jacob in Genesis 42:2: "Behold, I have heard that there is corn in Egypt," he tells his sons, and admonishes them to "Get you down thither, and buy for us from thence." A modern version: "My alimony check arrived today; there's corn in Egypt, so let's go to lunch at the '21' Club."

SEE ALSO "ALL THE TEA IN CHINA"

CORNY

This word has fallen out of common use, yet corniness still abounds, and no word as apt has risen to take its place.

COST A PRETTY PENNY

Expensive. An old phrase usually said rather snippily: "Did you see her fur coat? *That* must have cost a pretty penny!"

fig. 7: THAT'S THE STUFF

COXY-LOXY

Drunk, but in a good-natured way.

CRACK A TIDY CRUST

An old English phrase meaning "to achieve a success-ful life; have a commodious income," according to one vintage dictionary. Those who merely "cracked the crust" made a sufficient income, but had "nothing to write home about" (see page 141).

CRACKERS

"Crackers," "bananas," "fruitcake," and "nuts": the old-fashioned synonyms for the word "crazy" make that state of mind seem highly edible.

SEE ALSO "'CRAZY FOR YOU': OLD-FASHIONED LABELS FOR THE MENTALLY UNSOUND" (FACING PAGE)

CRAW

"Craw" = "stomach." Something that got figuratively "stuck in your craw" was a situation that you couldn't digest, something that bothered or annoyed you. ("The nerve of that man! He tells everyone that *he* discovered me. Boy, does that stick in my craw.")

CRAZY FOR YOU

Old-Fashioned Labels for the Mentally Unsound

It's relatively astonishing how many slang terms there are for the condition of "madness," many of which add a veneer of levity.

Bananas	Mad as a hatter
Bats in the belfry	Mad as a March hare
Batty	Nuts / nutty
Bonkers	Off one's rocker
Crackers	Out to lunch
Dotty	'Round the bend
Fruity / fruitcake	Screwy / screw loose
Kook / kooky	Snap one's twig
Loon / loony	Touched
Loopy	

CREAM OF THE VALLEY

A nineteenth-century Americanism for "gin." Colorfully illustrated in a rambling, bizarre 1839 short story called "Some Account of Himself by the Irish Oyster Eater":

> The orange-woman expressed a decided opinion, that a drop of cream of the valley would do her all the good in the world, enquiring of your humble servant in the same breath, whether I had ever, in my life, tasted cream of the valley. 'Why . . . 'tis nothing at all but the sweetest of mountain dew, wid roses and lilies in it,' [she exclaimed].

The "mountain dew" to which the "orange-woman" referred had nothing to do with today's sugar-bog soft drink; rather, it meant "whisky."

SEE ALSO "WHITE SATIN"

CROCODILE TEARS

An emphatically insincere show of sorrow, this centuries-old term stems from the ancient belief that crocodiles shed tears while chomping up their victims.

fig. 8: BAH! COLD TEA, STALE BREAD. MY YELP REVIEW IS WRITING ITSELF.

CROSS

A quaint and underused synonym for the more frequently invoked word "crabby."

CRUMBY

Lousy.

SEE ALSO "'I DAMN NEAR BROKE MY CRAZY NECK': THE MEMORABLE VOCABU- LARY AND PHRASEOLOGY OF HOLDEN CAULFIELD," PAGE 98

CRY OVER SPILLED MILK

To weep over useless regrets. Are you ever going to get that milk back into the glass? No, you shall not. So better to just forget about it and move on, *tout de suite*.

CRY ROAST MEAT

To boast about one's own good luck or fortune.

CRY UP

To ply someone with sycophantic praise. Also used as an adjective:

> I was prone to take disgust towards a girl so idolized and so cried up, as she was, by her aunt and her grandmother, and all their set.

—Jane Austen, *Emma* (1815)

CRY WOLF

To raise a false alarm, like the irritating little shepherd boy in Aesop's fable who regularly shouted "Wolf, wolf" to get his neighbors' attention. They would flock to his defense, only to find him quite wolfless. Somewhat predictably, one day a wolf meandered along, licking his chops; the shepherd "cried wolf" and no one came to his aid. Depending on who's recounting the tale, the wolf makes off with most of the sheep—and sometimes the shepherd himself.

"CRYING WOLF"

Still-Relevant Phrases from Aesop's Fables

What follows is a short list of popular Aesop-inspired idioms,
and the fables from which they originated. Although decidedly
old-fashioned, they still provide savvy insights into human nature
and should absolutely remain in our vernacular.

"Sour grapes"

From *The Fox and the Grapes*, in which a fox spots
a bunch of juicy grapes on a vine, but can't leap high
enough to reach them. He skulks away, telling himself
that the grapes were sure to be sour anyway. Any guy
who hasn't gotten the girl probably finds this to be a
familiar notion.

"Killing the golden goose"

From *The Goose That Laid the Golden Eggs*, in which a
couple owns a rather lucratively talented goose. Tired
of receiving only one golden egg a day, these gluttons
slay the bird and open it up, thinking that they can
get the whole stash at once. Instead of gold, they find
stinky old innards, as in any other goose. The idiom is
a metaphor for a shortsighted action that may seem to
bring an immediate reward, but will more likely have
unsavory long-term consequences.

"The lion's share"

A term from an eponymous fable in which a lion,
fox, jackal, and wolf go deer hunting. They kill a stag
and divide it into four parts. The lion claims the first
quarter because he's the so-called king of the beasts.
Then, as the other animals are about to tuck into their
deer hocks, the lion takes the second quarter as an
arbiter's fee of sorts. Next, he adds the third quarter to
his bloody pile to compensate for his part in the chase,
and the other animals are left to fight over the last
measly bit (although in some versions the lion takes all
four quarters). Therefore, "the lion's share" means the
largest portion of a whole.

CUCKOO

A peppery little synonym for "crazy"—or simply being crazy about something. ("I'm absolutely cuckoo about orangutans—can't get enough of them!")

CUNNING

I have a particular fondness for the word "cunning." I'd use it more except that whenever I do, people think I mean "crafty" or "conniving" when I'm invariably trying to describe something "cute" and "dear." (The usage seems to have changed around 1930 for some reason.) One of my favorite vintage cookbooks— 1917's *A Thousand Ways to Please a Husband*—is particularly profligate with the word: In the course of one hundred pages, little cupids on a Valentine's table, conical chicken croquettes, toast, the miniature hatchets in a Washington's birthday fondant log, and the butterflies adorning a luncheon place-card all rate the "c" treatment, as indeed they should. Yet nowadays, if you allude to a particularly cunning hat or cunning miniature deck of cards, people are apt to look at you with suspicion and confusion. Which is really too bad, because as technology becomes ever more minute, it's a term whose time has come—I can't think of a better adjective for an iPhone, personally.

SADIE STEIN • DEPUTY EDITOR, *THE PARIS REVIEW*

CURTAINS

The end, as in death or ruin. ("When Dad discovers that I crashed his car again, it'll be curtains for me.") The phrase referred to the closing of curtains across a stage following the end of an act or a play.

CUSHION-THUMPER

The best definition of this phrase belongs to *Grose's Classical Dictionary of the Vulgar Tongue* (1823): "A parson; many of whom in the fury of their eloquence, heartily belabour their cushions."

CUT A FINE FIGURE

To inspire admiration with your overwhelming elegance or appearance. Some sources say that this phrase was used largely for men ("Cecil cut a fine figure today in that seersucker suit and porkpie hat"), while young ladies "cut a dash" instead.

CUT THE CACKLE

I.e., quit horsing around and get down to business.

fig. 9: GENTLEMEN! DON'T MAKE ME BANG THIS TEENY GAVEL AGAIN

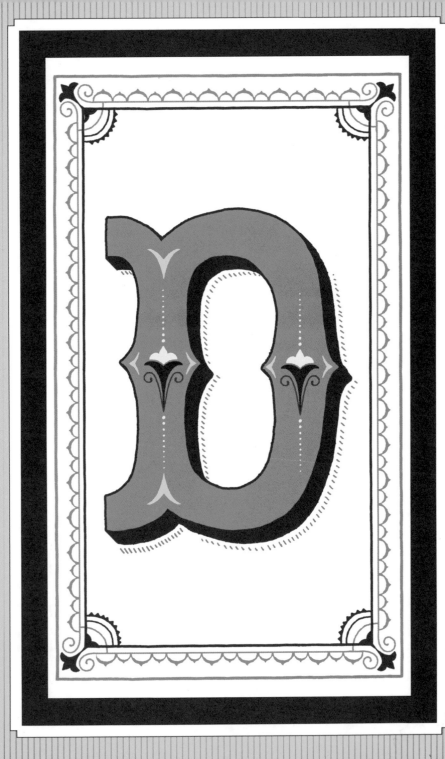

DADDY-O

Cooler-than-thou guys referred to each other as "daddy-o" from the 1920s through the 1960s. It was originally a jazz term: "You've got *chops*, daddy-o."

DAME

A slang word for "girl" or "lady." Used wonderfully by Humphrey Bogart, who, in the 1941 film *High Sierra,* quipped: "I wouldn't give you two cents for a dame without a temper."

DANDIPRAT

This sixteenth-century word just *sounds* insulting, and indeed, it is: "dandiprat" means a "silly, finicky, or puerile person."

DANGED

A prudish-yet-fun mid-century alternative to "I'll be damned." ("I'll be danged if I fall for one of his corny lines again!")

DAPPER

Taken in their totality, the various meanings of this old-fashioned word conjure up a very specific creature:

> **dap·per** \'dap-ər\ *adj* **1** : neat; trim; smart **2** : lively and brisk **3** : small and active

One imagines a neat, trim, small man, taking brisk little steps up the street, dusting off his lapel and straightening his tie as he goes; he wears a hat, of course. Such a man would always turn up to a date with a bouquet of flowers and give a little bow at the door.

DARK HORSE

An unlikely competitor about whom little is known. Various sources assert that the term emerged between 1825 and the 1840s; according to the *American Heritage Dictionary of Idioms,*

> This metaphoric expression originally alluded to an unknown horse
> winning a race and was so used in a novel by Benjamin Disraeli
> (*The Young Duke*, 1831). It soon began to be transferred to political
> candidates, among the first of whom was James K. Polk.
> He won the 1844 Democratic presidential nomination on the
> eighth ballot and went on to win the election.

The exact use of the word in Disraeli's novel was as follows: "A dark horse, which had never been thought of . . . rushed past the grandstand in sweeping triumph." And for decades ever after, the term was used to describe everyone from improbable romantic suitors to uppity businessmen vying for prominence.

SEE ALSO "ALSO-RAN"

DARN TOOTIN'

An old-fashioned, Looney Tunes-esque way of saying, "Damn straight!"

DASTARDLY

This pleasing 1500s adjective ("mean; cowardly") also conveniently comes in noun form: "dastard" ("a mean, sneaking coward"). Use it as a surprising alternative to the overused "bastard" when describing a man of ill repute.

DEAD AS A DOORNAIL

Meaning really, really dead. Not just a little bit dead. *Utterly* dead. Just why a doornail is being cited as an example of deadness—as opposed to, say, a door*knob*—is unclear, but the term has been around forever. Even Shakespeare saw fit to include it in at least one of his works, *King Henry IV*: ". . . [If] I do not leave you all as dead as a doornail, I pray God I may never eat grass more."

DEAD SEA FRUIT

Anything that appears tempting and gorgeous-looking, but once obtained turns out to have been a disappointing, even bitter, illusion. A reference to fabled fruits that once grew near ancient Sodom, which "have a color as if they were fit to be eaten, but if you pluck them with your hands, they dissolve into smoke and ashes" (Titus Flavius Josephus, 37 AD–c. 100 AD).

DEAR

I know what happened to "Dear So-and-so." After e-mail came along, people found themselves writing more and more notes to strangers. They got scared that "dear" sounded like—well, like an endearment (or, heaven forfend, a come-on). They needn't have worried. As the OED beautifully explains: "The earlier sense was of 'esteemed, valued,' rather than 'loved,' but the passage of the one notion into the other is too gradual to admit of their separation." That ambiguity is what makes "dear" so universally appropriate. "Dear Mom" is affectionate. "Dear Sir" is formal. "Dearest enemy" is Shakespearian. "Dear Mr. Doe" is just polite.

LORIN STEIN • EDITOR, *THE PARIS REVIEW*

DEVIL AND THE DEEP BLUE SEA

Linguistically speaking, if you found yourself "between" these entities, you were said to be vacillating between two deeply unpleasant and dangerous situations.

DEVIL-MAY-CARE

Reckless; rash. Often used to describe someone's cavalier attitude or approach to life: "She spends money in a frightfully devil-may-care manner."

fig. 10: ROLL 'EM

DEVIL'S TEETH

Seventeenth-century slang for "dice," which were alternatively known as "Devil's bones." Cards were, of course, also considered part of Lucifer's realm, and earned the moniker "Devil's books."

DEW-DRINK

A wee little drink nipped before breakfast—i.e., when dew still festoons the grass outside.

DICK

An old-guard word for "detective." Hotel staff detectives—now a largely obsolete profession—were known as "house dicks." You can see why *that* term went out of fashion.

THE DICKENS

A centuries-old euphemism for "Devil," which was used in a whole host of exclamations: "What the dickens?", "You scared the dickens out of me!", "That hurts like the dickens!", and so on.

DIG A WELL NEAR THE RIVER

To do something moronic.

DILLY-DALLY

To loiter around aimlessly; trifle along.

DINGBAT

As recently as the 1970s, this word signified a "silly or empty-headed person" (fans of the sitcom *All in the Family* will recall that this was Archie Bunker's default term of endearment for his wife, Edith), and it still makes quite a gratifying insult. Yet since its emergence in the 1800s, "dingbat" has also been used to describe "money" ("I ain't got a dingbat to spare!"), a "professional tramp" ("That dingbat is loitering around our porch again, hiccupping and bellowing out show tunes"), and "an alcoholic drink" ("I'll have a double dingbat on the rocks, pronto").

DINNER SET

An old-guard term for "teeth." Would be especially apt today, considering that many of this era's Hollywood stars and starlets have swapped out their real teeth for gleamingly white, plate-sized *objets*. *The Dictionary of Slang and Colloquial English* (1905) offers this funny example of usage: "Your dinner set wants looking to, you need to go to the dentist."

fig. 11: BITE ME

DIM BULBS and DOPES

*Old-fangled Honorifics
for Less-than-Bright Individuals*

History's dumbbells inspired a whole host
of colorful monikers, including:

Addlepate	Lunkhead
Blockhead	Meathead
Booby	Muttonhead
Chowderhead	Nincompoop
Chump	Numbskull
Dimwit	Pea brain
Dolt	Pinhead
Duffer	Simpleton
Dunce	Stooge
Fathead	Tomfool
Goosecap	Twit

DIPSTICK

"Dipstick" is another one of those nouns that had no business falling out of fashion. Official definitions claim that it means "a fool or jerk," but the term is far more nuanced than that. A close synonym: "weenie," or "an insignificant, disliked person." Weenies and dipsticks were generally considered inept and malleable; such "dippy" creatures still exist by the barrelful today, and they certainly require appropriate words to describe them. The modern variation "dipshit" is too coarse and therefore doesn't evoke the same mild wienery-ness.

DIRTY DOUBLE-CROSSER

A schoolyard-ish phrase for "traitor." Similarly pleasing, old-fashioned synonyms: "two-timer" and "double-dealer."

SEE ALSO "SNAKE IN THE GRASS"

DOGGERY

A saloon:

> So me and the duke went up to the village, and hunted around there for the king, and by-and-by we found him in the back room of a little low doggery, very tight, and a lot of loafers bullyragging him for sport, and he a-cussing and a-threatening with all his might, and so tight he couldn't walk, and couldn't do nothing to them.

—Mark Twain, *The Adventures of Huckleberry Finn* (1884)

DOLL

Slang for a pretty girl or lady. One source says that the term dates back to the 1500s, when it was an "endearing name for a female pet or a mistress." Also used as a form of address ("Let's go paint the town red, doll"), along with its sister expression, "doll-face."

SEE ALSO "DAME"

DOLLED UP

Dressed in a particularly showy—even garish—manner:

I once saw a group of little girls on a Mississippi sidewalk, all dolled up in their mothers' and sisters' cast-off finery, old raggedy ball gowns and plumed hats and high-heeled slippers, enacting a meeting of ladies in a parlor with a perfect mimicry of polite Southern gush and simper.

—Tennessee Williams, *Person-to-Person* (1955)

DOMINOES

Another entertaining old-fashioned term for teeth.

SEE ALSO "DINNER SET"

DONE AND DUSTED

Successfully completed.

DON'T BRUISE YOUR KNUCKLES

In other words, don't even bother knocking—as demonstrated in a description of John's and Jane's restaurant in Al Hirschfeld's book, *The Speakeasies of 1932* :

The booths are small, but comfortable, and no objection to propping up the bar if you prefer to pass out perpendicularly . . . Never open before dinner time, so don't bruise your knuckles.

DON'T TAKE ANY WOODEN NICKELS

An American idiom from the early 1900s, meaning "Don't let yourself get ripped off," and sometimes simply, "Don't do anything stupid."

DOSE OF THE BALMY

To go to sleep ("I'm off for a dose of the balmy").

SEE ALSO "CATCH FORTY WINKS"

DOUBLE-JUGGS

Buttocks.

DOWN THE ROAD

An old-fashioned term for "slave to fashion." A "down the road chap" is overly modish; stylish; a follower on the path of voguish apparel.

DOWNSTAIRS

Hell. ("Going downstairs? See you there shortly.")

DRAGON'S TEETH

Any action that will bring future destruction; also known as "seeds of strife." This expression comes from a Greek myth in which Phoenician prince Cadmus slaughters a dragon and, at the urging of Athena, plants some of its teeth in the ground. In due course, the teeth sprout into a murderous clan of warriors. Lesson learned.

DRAT

A quaint exclamation upon hearing rotten news, "drat" is a first cousin to the equally quaint utterance "rats." The comeback-worthy adjective "dratted" means "damned" or "confounded." ("How does this dratted credit card always manage to max itself out?")

SEE ALSO "BLASTED"

BENDERS IN BYGONE ERAS

Historical Euphemisms for "Drunk"

Over the centuries, scores of colorful words and phrases
have been coined to describe the sometimes-joyous,
often-ignoble state of inebriation. A small sampling:

Back teeth afloat

Banged up to the eyes

Bent

Blind

Blotto

Can't see a hole in a ladder

Dull-eyed

Fogged

Full of Dutch courage

Gone a peg too low

Half-seas-over

Holding up the lamppost

In bed with one's boots on

In drink

In one's cups

In the suds

On a jag

On a tear

On a toot

Ossified

Pickled

Pie-eyed

Razzle-dazzled

Seeing two moons

Sozzled

Spifflicated

Stewed

Stinko

Three sheets to the wind

(*Note: the number of sheets
cited varies*)

Tight

Tip merry

Tying one on

Zozzled

DREAMBOAT

A very Marilyn Monroe-esque word; one imagines it was always uttered in breathless tones ("He's such a dreamboat that I positively drool every time I clap eyes on him"). Be sure to revive also its adjective form: "dreamy."

DRIP

The formal definition of this currently underused word says it all: "An insipid, inane person." I.e., a close relative of the "dipstick" (see page 57).

DRUMSTICKS

A delectable vintage word for "legs."

SEE ALSO "GAMS"

DRUTHERS

I love asking persons their druthers. Grammatically, what's your druther sounds to my ear like what's your problem, or what's your poison. Druther — a collapse of "I'd rather" — is a gate-way word that optimally points to other more luminous possibilities. Druthers for hydrangea over peonies. Druthers for *Melancholia* over *Tree of Life*. Druthers for croquet over miniature golf.

MICHAEL D. SNEDIKER • POET; CRITIC;
AUTHOR OF *QUEER OPTIMISM*, *NERVOUS PASTORAL*, AND *BOURDON*

DRY UP

In the mid-1800s, if you were droning on about a topic of no interest to anyone but yourself, someone might have advised you to "dry up." It's absolutely worth resurrecting this term, which *sounds* somewhat more polite than "shut up"—and yet manages to be even more insulting.

DUCKY

"Isn't that just *ducky*." Anyone who spat out this sentence during its mid-century heyday likely did so with the deepest sarcasm. Make sure to watch the 1942 film *The Man Who Came to Dinner,* in which the main character—an über-acerbic critic named Sheridan Whiteside—utters the word with more acidity than anyone else in the history of mankind.

SEE ALSO "GRAND" *and* "SWELL"

DULL AS DISHWATER

Just picture a sink filled with dreary, lukewarm suds, and you'll appreciate the aptness of this old-guard phrase. Another equally dreary version: "dull as *ditch* water."

DUMB-FOOZLED

Confused; perplexed. Delightful as a verb, too: "As a child, I took great pleasure in dumb-foozling my teachers, baby-sitters, and therapists."

SEE ALSO "COMFOOZLED"

fig. 12: WHEN DO I ADD THE EYE OF NEWT...?

DYED-IN-THE-WOOL

Another offering from the agrarian 1500s, "dyed-in-the-wool" means "permanent" or "through-and-through." ("My Uncle Barnaby is a dyed-in-the-wool Judy Garland fan.")

DYNAMITE

A somewhat explosive compliment, usually uttered by aggressively enthusiastic people in the 1970s: "Wow, this fondue is really dynamite!"

EARWIGGING

Some definitions say that this very old word meant a "scolding" or
"harangue"; others insist that it was only a true earwigging if the rebuke
was made in private.

SEE ALSO "BATTY-FANGING"

EASY STREET

A nirvana-like state of luxury and financial security, memorably commemo-
rated by the song "Easy Street" in the 1977 Broadway show *Annie*. According
to notorious, Depression-era orphanage proprietor Miss Hannigan and her
ne'er-do-well brother Rooster, "Easy Street" is a place that's "like no other."
One doesn't get there "by playing from the rule book"; instead, you "stack
the aces" and "load the dice." Your reward once you hit Easy Street? You get
to "sleep all day" and play with the other "rich folks."

EAT HUMBLE PIE

Being forced to apologize or admit the errors of one's ways, usually in the
face of humiliation. A variety of sources assert that the phrase somehow
managed to evolve from "numble pie" (sometimes called "umble pie"), a
dish made from deer innards that was popular from the 1400s through the
1600s. Other variations: "eat one's words," and "eat crow."

EAT THE AIR

A Shakespearian phrase, meaning "to be deluded with false hopes," *à la* poor
old Hamlet: "I eat the air, promise-crammed; you cannot feed capons so."

EGGS IS EGGS

"Decidedly" or "assuredly." ("Those pearls are fake, sure as eggs is eggs.")

EIGHTY-SIX

A Prohibition-era term; to "eighty-six" someone meant to boot him out of a bar or restaurant. The likely origin: the now-extinct but still-legendary Chumley's, a one-time speakeasy that kept a whole bevy of writers, poets, and journalists—including William Faulkner, Eugene O'Neill, and Edna St. Vincent Millay—afloat in the 1920s. Chumley's was located at 86 Bedford Street in Manhattan's Greenwich Village, and when a police raid was nigh, patrons were told to "eighty-six it out the garden door."

ELBOW CROOKER

An aggressive drinker. Not to be confused with an "elbow scraper" (fiddler) or an "elbow shaker" (gambler).

ETERNITY BOX

Coffin.

fig. 13: DO NOT DISTURB

IMPOSED EXILE

How Old-Timers Got Rid of Unwanted Parties

It appears that pestiness is a time-honored tradition. Our ancestors sent annoying people packing by hissing one of the following phrases:

Be off with you	Go saw your timber
Beat it	Kiss off
Bug off	Scram
Buzz off	Shoo
Get lost	Skedaddle
Git	Sling your hook
Go fly a kite	Sweep on
Go pick your nose	Take a hike

FACE TO THE WALL

Nearing the end of life.

FAIR to MIDDLING [and OTHER OHIOISMS]

My head is full of expressions piled up from my background—mine and all my American ancestors—in Ohio. In my family, we used them continually and casually in everyday speech (my father was especially eloquent—and funny—with them) and they tend to crop up in my stories without my even having to reach for them. Favorites include: "Raise a ruckus," meaning "make a noisy fuss"; "kit and caboodle," meaning "everything big and small"; and my favorite, "fair to middling," meaning "only average." Maybe they're common to every location these days, but I hope not! I like to think they still belong to Ohio.

NATALIE BABBITT • NEWBERY HONOR AWARD-WINNING AUTHOR OF *TUCK EVERLASTING* AND *THE DEVIL'S STORYBOOK*

FAL-LALS

A late-1800s definition of this word is as delightful as the word itself: "trumpery ornaments." Later definitions clarify matters: "a bit of finery" and "a showy bit of dress." Also make sure to revive its sister noun, "fallalery."

FAR OUT

As in, "groovy"; "cool." ("All of his front teeth are gold? That's far out, man.")

FAREWELL

Such a poignant and lovely way to say "goodbye."

FEEL LIKE A MILLION DOLLARS

To feel great. Or, more snappily phrased: "feel [or look] like a million *bucks*."

FELLOW

Supplanted in today's vernacular by the word "guy," the word "fellow" has more affability and elegance. ("He carried my packages all the way home and refused a tip—what a lovely fellow.")

FIB

This grandmotherly word dates back to the 1500s; one source asserts that "fib" is short for "fibble-fable," a "gradational compound based on [the word] fable." It's wonderful both as a noun ("She always tells the most transparent fibs") and a verb ("She is well known for fibbing about absolutely everything"). Another great variation: "She could be a professional *fibber*."

FIDDLE-DEE-DEE

An old expression of dismissive scorn. The most famous utterer of this phrase was, of course, *Gone with the Wind* protagonist Scarlett O'Hara. As she says in the 1939 film:

> "Marriage, fun? Fiddle-dee-dee. Fun for men, you mean."

FIDDLE-FADDLE

And speaking of "fibble-fable" (see "fib" above), here's another derivative that should be revived. The quaint term "fiddle-faddle" means "nonsense." Yet in some circles, the phrase accrued some unlikely racy connotations. While in the White House, President John F. Kennedy employed two young secretaries who were dubbed "Fiddle" and "Faddle" by the Secret Service; some JFK biographers assert that he was partial to Fiddle-Faddle threesomes and skinny-dipping sessions in the White House pool.

FIDDLESTICKS

As in, "Fiddlesticks! That's the third piece of toast I've burned this morning." Also used as a term of dismissal: "I don't care a fiddlestick what that old biddy says."

SEE ALSO "CARE A FIG"

FIEND

Employ this currently underused Middle English word when describing people of unspeakable evil: "My fiend of a landlord raised my rent *again*."

FIGURE

This mid-century word for "body" should always be paired with contemporaneous adjectives: "She's got a perfectly *marvelous* figure—look at that tiny waist!" or "You don't have to worry about any competition from her: after all, she's got a *lousy* figure."

FIMBLE-FAMBLE

A nineteenth-century phrase for a "lame, prevaricating excuse."

FINE WORDS BUTTER NO PARSNIPS

Promises alone don't guarantee results.

> Who was the blundering idiot who said that
> "fine words butter no parsnips"? Half the parsnips of society
> are served and rendered palatable with no other sauce.

—William Thackeray, *Vanity Fair* (1848)

FINK

A contemptible person. One fluent user of the word: the father in the classic children's novel *Harriet the Spy*, who launches into the following speech after a hard day at work: "Finks, finks, double-barreled rat, rat, rat, finks, finks, finks . . . you wouldn't *believe* the iniquity . . . you will not *believe* when I tell you the unmitigated *finkiness* of those guys." The response of his wife, who was presumably used to such tirades: "Darling, here, have your drink."

Also great: the phrase "fink out," or withdraw one's support.

FIRKYTOODLE

To cuddle or fondle. ("Let's make margaritas and firkytoodle in front of the fire.")

FIRST CHOP

I.e., first rate; of highest excellence. *The Dictionary of English Idiomatic Phrases* (1891) claims that this was an "Anglo-Chinese expression."

FISTICUFFS

A fancier old word for "fistfight." The term also mutated into the still-useful "fisticuffer."

FIT AS A FIDDLE

A 1600s phrase for "in perfect health." Earlier versions of the saying include "fine as a fiddle" and "right as a fiddle."

FIT TO BE TIED

Livid; wildly angry. Likely comes from the practice of "tying down" or restraining an out-of-control person.

FIZZING

Meaning "excellent; first-rate." Especially nice because it evokes Champagne, and anything that evokes Champagne is revival-worthy.

SEE ALSO "FIRST CHOP"

FLASH IN THE PAN

A short-lived success, despite a "flashy" or promising start. Many sources have speculated that the phrase originated during the California Gold Rush, when creek-bound prospectors would get excited to see a glimmer in their pans, only to be disappointed when the source of the flash wasn't real gold after all. Sounds like a perfectly sensible explanation—yet other sources assert that the term is even older. *The Phrase Finder* places its birth era as the late seventeenth century, and offers the following convincing exposition:

> Flintlock muskets used to have small pans to hold charges of gunpowder. An attempt to fire the musket in which the gunpowder flared up without a bullet being fired was a "flash in the pan."

FLIBBERTYJIBBET

This word is so much sweeter and more appealing than its contemporary equivalents: I refer, of course, to skank, ho, or hoochie.

SIMON DOONAN • AUTHOR OF *ECCENTRIC GLAMOUR* AND *GAY MEN DON'T GET FAT*

FLIMFLAM

A sham story. As a verb, to deceive: "We flimflammed our way out of a speeding ticket last night."

FLIP ONE'S WIG

A far more amusing variation on "flip one's lid," i.e., to lose control or fly into a rage.

FLUNKY

A yes-man, also known in the old days as a "toady."

FLY-CATCHER

The definition given by the 1905 *Dictionary of Slang and Colloquial English* is harsher than the word itself: "An open-mouthed ignoramus; a Gape-seed."

FOLLOW-ME-LADS

A curtain of alluring, scented curls bobbing about on a lady's shoulder. Also called "kissing-strings."

FOO-FOO

An insignificant person. Or, as Oscar Wilde would have put it, a woman of no importance.

FOP

This word is a gift from late Middle English, and describes a "man who is excessively vain and concerned about his dress, appearance, and manners." Characters who originally personi- fied "foppishness" include Sir Fopling Flutter and Lord Foppington, both fictional products of Restoration comedies in the late 1600s. Since the word was considered pejorative, it was often coupled with adjectives like "useless" and "heart- less." It also gave rise to the term "fop-doodle," i.e., a fool.

GIVE US THIS DAY OUR DAILY BREAD

A Smattering of Old Words for "Food"

The terms listed below clearly belonged to the realm of
casual dining; one can hardly imagine a "tippybob" (see page 196)
like Gilded Age society doyenne Caroline Astor inviting her
contemporaries over for some "chow," after all.

Bacon

Board

Grub

Mess

Nosh

Slop(s)

Stomach-timber

Tuck

Vittles

FOUR-FLUSHER

We all know a four-flusher: a bluffer, someone who makes "false or pretentious claims." The nineteenth-century term clearly has its roots in the game of poker, and indicated a situation in which a player claimed that he had a flush—a poker hand with five cards all of one suit—when in reality, he only had four cards of one suit.

FOX'S SLEEP

Everyone knows that a fox sleeps with one eye open. A person "in a fox's sleep" is, by extension, feigning indifference to what's happening around him, yet is keeping a watchful eye on the goings-on.

FOXY

Fetching in a somewhat dangerous way. Also: "slyly clever; tricky." The poster boy of foxiness—in both senses of the word—appears to be Donald Draper, main character of the period television drama *Mad Men*, which chronicles the hijinks of naughty advertising execs in the 1960s. The chiseled, taciturn Don is a liar and adulterer supreme—and yet cleverly manages to lure all sorts of adoring, soft critters into his fox's lair.

FRESH OUT OF A BANDBOX

Another one of those old phrases with two wildly different meanings. The first: having a "smart or neat appearance." One source states that this seventeenth-century term alludes to the boxes in which neckbands and hats were stored. To be "fresh out of a bandbox" implied a crispness associated with a new hat or tie.

However, in America, the word "bandbox" later became slang for a local prison. One who was "fresh from the bandbox" in this context was hardly likely to seem "smart," "neat," or "fresh."

FROWSY

A powdery way of calling someone or something "dumpy" or "slovenly."

FRUITCAKE

A crazy person—but someone whose insanity is of the "kooky" rather than violent variety. ("Old Aunt Petunia is such a fruitcake: she always wears a Santa hat, even on her annual trips to Aruba.")

FUBSEY

Plump. ("That fubsey wench clearly lives on meat, potatoes, and ale.")

FUDDY DUDDY

Do you happen to know any old-fashioned, stuffy, conservative men? If so, you are acquainted with a "fuddy duddy." Let's call them by their proper name again.

SEE ALSO "FUSSBUDGET" *and* "STUFFED SHIRT"

FULL FEATHER

When one is gaily dressed, he or she is "in full feather."

FULL OF HOT AIR

Term describing a four-flusher (see facing page).

fig. 14: THANK YOU BUT I'D RATHER NOT

FUNNY FISH

An eccentric. Other animal kingdom synonyms: "odd duck," "odd bird," "queer duck," "lone wolf," and "fish out of water."

FUSSBUDGET

Someone who needlessly fusses or frets. The term has several wonderful siblings as well: "fusspot" and "fussbox."

GADABOUT

Contemporary definitions state that a "gadabout" is a person who flits restlessly from one locale or social activity to another. Yet an earlier source—*A Dictionary of Slang and Colloquial English* (1905)—offers a more amusing description: "A trapesing gossip; as a housewife seldom seen at home, but very often at her neighbours' doors."

GALLANT

1. Brave, spirited, noble-minded, or chivalrous.

2. Exceptionally polite and attentive to women; courtly.

3. Stately; grand.

No wonder this word went out of fashion; there are too few men today to whom it applies.

GALLOWS-RIPE

Someone who's just *looking* for trouble and ready for the gallows rope. Also clever: "gallowsness," which means "recklessness; mischievousness."

GALOOT

An uncouth person. ("The third-generation Vanderbilts might have *acted* like they were America's royalty, but ol' Cornelius Vanderbilt was apparently quite a galoot.")

GALOPTIOUS

An expression of delight: "This songbird pie is simply galoptious!"

GAMS

Drumsticks (see page 61).

GAMCASES

Stockings.

GASCONADING

We must bring back the word "gasconading"—which means "extravagant boasting" or "blustering." It fits so many politicians' antics today.

COKIE ROBERTS • POLITICAL COMMENTATOR;
JOURNALIST; AUTHOR OF *FOUNDING MOTHERS* AND *LADIES OF LIBERTY*

GASSER

Braggart. A slightly more modern synonym: "gasbag."

GATHER WOOL

To dawdle; idle away; daydream. Not only should we bring back the phrase, but we should bring back the leisure time for such luxurious activities.

SEE ALSO "MOONRAKE"

GET A WIGGLE ON

More 1920s slang. The one means: put some pep in your step. Hustle along.

GET DOWN TO BRASS TACKS

When someone orders you to "get down to brass tacks," they're demanding that you muster courage and face the hard facts at hand. The origin of the phrase remains unclear, although some sources agree that it's likely a product of nineteenth-century America. One theory: that the brass tacks in question may refer to tacks used in haberdasheries, where cloth was measured between brass tacks hammered into the top of the shop's counter. How that could have evolved into the tough-love expression above is anyone's guess.

GET FRESH

To act in a brazen or impudent manner. ("If you get fresh with me, pal, I'll give you a bunch-of-fives in the nose.")

GET ONE'S DANDER UP

To become irritated or mad. Hollywood producer Samuel Goldwyn—who should be as famous for his hilarious, unlikely-genius quotes as the great Yogi Berra—reportedly misquoted this phrase frequently: "This makes me so sore it gets my dandruff up."

GET ONE'S GOAT

Another silly old saying that means to make someone angry. And, as everyone knows, there's nothing worse than an ornery goat. Unless, of course, you are dealing with an ornery horse. While the origin of the phrase has not been agreed upon, it is often asserted that it comes from racetrack culture. Horse trainers often placed goats into stalls alongside racehorses for a little bit of calming camaraderie. If a rival or ill-wisher removed the goat, the horse might get upset and perform badly in the race.

GET THE DRIFT

As in, "You keep messin' around with the boss's wife, we're gonna break your kneecaps—get the drift?"

GET THE FUZZY END OF THE LOLLIPOP

I.e., get a bum deal. Just ask Marilyn Monroe, who utters the phrase with gusto as Sugar Kane Kowalczyk in *Some Like It Hot* (1959): "All the girls drink; it's just that I'm the one that gets caught. Story of my life: I always get the fuzzy end of the lollipop." And as we all know, Monroe ultimately ended up getting the fuzzy end of the lollipop offscreen as well.

GET UP ON THE WRONG SIDE OF THE BED

To wake up in a terribly grumpy mood. Apparently this phrase goes back to ancient Rome. One imagines that Caligula—with all of his infamous late-night romps—must have gotten up on the wrong side of the bed fairly regularly.

GIFT OF THE GAB

An ability to wow listeners with your seamless and convincing oratory.

fig. 15: HOURS OF FUN

GIGAMAREE

A fun-to-say word for "a pretty but useless toy." "Gimcrack" is also a revival-worthy synonym.

GIGGLE WATER

Booze.

GILD THE PILL

To sugarcoat; to make something unappealing somehow seem attractive. ("That coat's made from possum, not mink: don't try to gild the pill!")

GINGER-SNAP

A quick-tempered person.

GIVE A HOOT

G-rated version of "Give a damn." To behold the phrase's amusing qualities, consider this "Disneyfied" line from the 1939 film *Gone with the Wind*:

RHETT
Frankly, my dear, I don't give a hoot.

SEE ALSO "CARE A FIG"

GIVEN THE GO-BY

Stood up at the altar: "Mitch gave poor old Mildred the go-by."

GLAD RAGS

Another lively term from the 1920s, meaning "dressy, glamorous clothes." Or in the parlance of the times, "ritzy" clothes.

GLIMFLASHY

Enraged; fuming away. ("I wouldn't ask him for money right now; he's still glimflashy about the other hundred bucks you owe him.")

GLUMP

It sounds like it should be a noun, but "glump" was actually a wonderfully pleasing verb, meaning "to sulk." "Glumpish"—an adjective—described someone with "a stubborn, sulky temperament."

GO JUMP IN A LAKE

A well-bred old way of telling someone to go to hell.

GO PLACES

To succeed. ("That kid's gonna go places. Not because she's talented, but because she's shameless.")

GO TO THE OLD NICK

A slightly less well-bred way of telling someone to go to hell.

GO-ALONG

A fool—clearly the sort who mindlessly follows the herd.

GOBSMACKED and GOBBEDLYGOOK

Leave it to a lipstick queen to be fascinated with the goings-on of the "gob." "Gobsmacked" is an old word that truly sounds like how it feels. To be "Gobsmacked" is to be shocked, momentarily frozen with disbelief and fascinated all at once. "Gobbedlygook" is another old-fashioned, visceral word that manages to sound like what it means. Dismissive and delightful to say, to declare something "Gobbedlygook" is annihilation at its most lyrical.

POPPY KING • AUTHOR OF *LESSONS OF A LIPSTICK QUEEN*

GOLDBRICK

Early 1900s slang for something that looks expensive but turns out to be worthless (i.e., a brick painted to look like it's made of gold). "Goldbricker" denotes someone—particularly a soldier—who shirks his or her duties, an idler.

SEE ALSO "DEAD SEA FRUIT"

GOLLUMPUS

A lumbering, clumsy lad: "I see that gollumpering gollumpus gollump down the street every day." An equally descriptive synonym: "gilly-gaupus."

GOLLY

And also: "gosh."

GOOD GRIEF

An exclamation denoting surprise or dismay, popularized by Charlie Brown and the other characters in Charles Schulz's "Peanuts" comic strip.

GOOD RIDDANCE TO BAD RUBBISH

An utterance expressing great joy about being free of some rankling individual or situation (i.e., the "rubbish" part of the equation). *The Phrase Finder* asserts that Shakespeare is the likely coiner of the phrase "good riddance," which appears in his *Troilus and Cressida* (circa 1602):

THERSITES:
I will see you hanged, like clotpoles, ere I come any more to your tents:
I will keep where there is wit stirring and leave the faction of fools.
[Exits]

PATROCLUS:
A good riddance.

An equally delightful term in this excerpt: the insult "clotpole"—but that is a different affair altogether.

SEE ALSO "HEAVE-HO"

"GOOD" SALUTATIONS

As in "good morning" and "good night": let's revive the whole range, including "good day," "good afternoon," and "good evening." Speakers of the romance languages still use their versions all of these phrases; they sound just as mannerly in English.

GOOD-TIME CHARLIE

Mid-century slang for a man purely devoted to the pursuit of pleasure and merry-making. The phrase was invoked in the iconic 1960 film *The Apartment* to describe character C. C. Baxter, whose neighbors believe him to be the ultimate ladies' man. In one scene, a neighbor admonishes Baxter's troubled love interest, played by a young Shirley MacLaine:

> You listen to me, you find yourself a nice, substantial man—
> a widower maybe—and settle down—instead of gnashing all those sleeping
> pills—for what, for whom? For some good-time Charlie?

GOOD-WOOLED

Of the highest merit; unflinchingly courageous.

GOODY-GOODY

Someone who is "cloyingly good," and therefore rightfully reviled. The expression may also be adorned with an optional "two shoes" at the end.

GOODY GOODY GUMDROPS

An exclamation best used sarcastically, upon hearing less-than-stellar news.

GOOSE IT UP

I.e., jazz things up. ("What is this, a monastery? Let's goose this party up a bit!")

GOOSE'S GAZETTE

A made-up tale; an untrue story; i.e., "a piece of reading for a goose."

GOOSECAP

One of the best old words for "a silly person" ever created.

GOT A LOT OF NERVE

Usually uttered by some tough broad recovering from a grievous wrong: "You got a lotta nerve, coming back here after runnin' away with that floozy."

GRAND

"She graduated from clown school at the top of her class—isn't that just *grand?*"

Another famous use of the word: instead of being called "Grandma," Jacqueline Kennedy Onassis was known to her grandchildren as "Grand Jackie." It's somewhat surprising that Marlene Dietrich—who was eventually forced to transition from a lifelong sex symbol to "the world's most famous grandmother"—didn't come up with this image-preserving honorific first.

A GREAT BEAUTY

This phrase is usually followed by the words "in her day." Appealing because it suggests beauty of a strong variety.

GREAT GUN

Nineteenth-century slang for a VIP, a big shot.

A GRAND OLD TIME

Vintage Terms for "Having a Blast"

Some of these expressions were not only used to describe lively events
and situations, but also lively people: "Oh, you simply *must*
ring up Agnes when you get to Chicago! She's a scream, I tell you."

A bang

A gas / gasser

A hoot

A hoot and a half

A riot

A scream

GREAT SNAKES!

A reaction upon hearing surprising news. Other variations include:

"GREAT SCOTT!"   "GREAT SHAKES!"

"GREAT SUN!"   "GREAT SMOKE!"

GREEDY GUTS

A particularly illustrative old-guard word for "a voracious or covetous person." And don't forget about "guzzle guts": someone who greedily suckles down booze.

SEE ALSO "ELBOW CROOKER"

GREEN AROUND THE GILLS

Looking ill, as though you were about to ralph all over the floor.

GROOVY

Ironically, before this term became synonymous with hippie flower-power, it used to be a nickname for a sardine. ("Give me a plate of groovies, a slab of bread, and a bucket of ale, mate.")

GUMMY

A toothless person.

GUNG HO

This fun old term, meaning "wholeheartedly enthusiastic," originally came from the Chinese term *gonghe*. It was picked up and "slangified" in the early 1940s by Carlson's Raiders, a World War II guerilla unit operating in the Pacific theater.

GUSSIED UP

Dolled up (see page 58).

HAIR-BUTCHER

A barber—presumably a distinctly ungifted one.

HANDSOME

Let's bring back this word to describe men
and women alike. One also used to see women
delightfully described in old debutante
announcements as "ornamental."

HANKY-SPANKY

Everyone likely still knows what "hanky-panky" means, thanks, in part,
to a Madonna song:

> *You better like hanky panky*
> *Nothing like a good spanky*

. . . but far fewer people today likely know about hanky-*spanky*. A man
of this description was fashionable, dashing, and exceedingly well-dressed:
"Just *look* at that hanky-spanky top hat and tails."

HAPPY AS A CLAM AT HIGH TIDE

The shorter version of this saying—"happy as a clam"—has long been
popular, but neither one offers any immediate explanation why clams in
particular are being cited as admirably jocular creatures. However, *The
Phrase Finder* offers a witty explanation: "High tide is when clams are free
from the attentions of predators; surely the happiest of times in the bivalve
mollusk world."

HARDY HAR HAR

A mid-century sarcastic response to something that isn't very funny ("Oh, that's a good one, all right—hardy har har.") Once favored by Jackie Gleason and Hanna-Barbera cartoon characters alike.

HAREBRAINED

This phrase has been describing reckless and scatterbrained people, notions, and schemes since the 1500s.

HARUM-SCARUM

Unpredictable; reckless: "That harum-scarum boy will poke his own eye out one of these days; mark my words." A less extreme, secondary definition: disorganized ("Her argument was as harum-scarum as the French army").

HASH

A hot mess: "You've made a pretty hash of that situation, haven't you?"

HEAVE-HO

As in, "give him the ol' heave-ho." The phrase implies the removal of an enormous weight, which is usually the case.

HEEBIE-JEEBIES

I.e., the "willies," the "jitters," the "creeps," or the "jimjams." Popularized during the 1920s.

HIGGLEDY-PIGGLEDY

In utter confusion and disorder, not unlike a pig pen.

HIGH AND MIGHTY

A derisive term to describe arrogant people of high social standing, usually used by people of lower ranking who would give anything to be high and mighty themselves if the opportunity presented itself. Also consider reviving this similar-sounding synonym: "highty-tighty."

HIGH HAT

Next time a pest approaches you at a party, give him or her the "high hat" instead of just "brushing him off" as usual. This might earn you the reputation of being "high-hatted" (snobbish), but at least you will be spared some annoyance.

HIJINKS

A term meaning "unrestrained fun" coined by people in the Jazz Age — and they knew what they were talking about in this department. The ultimate hijinks: Zelda and F. Scott Fitzgerald, Champagne-drunk and whooping it up in the Fifth Avenue fountain outside the Plaza Hotel.

HIVE

To rob. An enjoyable literary use of this work comes to us courtesy of Mark Twain, in *The Adventures of Huckleberry Finn*: "I felt so ornery and low down and mean that I says to myself, my mind's made up; I'll hive that money for them or bust."

HOGWASH and HOOEY

Charming Arcane Words for "Nonsense"

All of these phrases must be reintroduced immediately—
they are far more delightful than today's coarse synonym "bullshit."

Applesauce	Humbug
Baloney	Malarkey
Claptrap	Miff-maff
Fiddle-faddle	Mumbo jumbo
Flam	Piffle
Flapdoodle / Flamdoodle	Poppycock
Flumadiddle	Rimble-ramble
Fudge	Skittles
Gibble-gabble / Giffle-gaffle	Tilly-vally
Hokum	Trillibub
Hornswoggle	Twaddle
Horsefeathers	Whim-wham

HO-HUM

A cutting expression of boredom; a verbal yawn. ("You're proposing to me *again*? Ho-hum.")

HOCUS POCUS

A deception; a bamboozlement; chicanery. Known in French as *le hoax*.

HOGWASH

A deliciously dismissive exclamation upon hearing "hocus-pocus-y" news: "He told me that he's the sausage king of Texas, but that's hogwash."

HOLIDAY

The word "vacation" sounds bureaucratic. "Holiday" sounds like fun.

HOLY COW

Be sure to revive the following related "holy" exclamations as well:

HOLY CATFISH!	HOLY MOLEY!
HOLY MACARONI!	HOLY MOSES!
HOLY MACKEREL!	HOLY SMOKES!

Not that anyone has ever really accused a mackerel or blob of macaroni of being especially holy, but that, of course, is part of the fun.

HOOK OR BY CROOK

By fair means or foul. One explanation behind the idiom: burglars used to use hooks to steal things through open windows. A pretty low-concept approach, but, hey—whatever works.

HOOLIGAN

A delightful word for a distinctly undelightful entity: "a tough and aggressive or violent youth." It first appeared in London police-court reports in 1898 and was "almost certainly [derived] from the surname Houlihan, supposedly from a lively family of that name in London who figured in music hall songs of the decade," according to the Online Etymology Dictionary. Journalists picked up on the term and liked it enough to transmute it into various adjectives ("hooliganesque," "hooliganic") and a verb ("to hooligan").

HOOPTY-DO

A festive alternative to the plain old exclamation, "Hooray." ("We struck gold in them thar hills—hoopty-do!")

SEE ALSO "HUZZAH"

HOPPED UP

In a state of excitement, i.e., a good time to shout "Hoopty-do!"

fig. 16: IT'S FOR ME

HORN

The telephone. ("Harold, your no-goodnik, rotten scamp of a son is on the horn!")

HORSE AROUND

To cavort; carry on; roughhouse. Don't forget about "horseplay," or "rough, boisterous play."

HORSE FEATHERS

I.e., "bunk," "malarkey," "flimflam," "tomfoolery," and "twaddle." In other words, a synonym for "nonsense." It was also the title of a 1932 Marx Brothers film—which was rife with horse-featherish tomfoolery and flimflam of the highest caliber.

HOT

Stolen: "That Rolex is hotter than hell in August!"

HOT DIGGITY DOG

Another amusing exclamation of exultation: "I just won a hundred bucks with a scratch-off lottery card—hot diggity dog!"

A HOT ONE

A lie. Related, of course, to "full of hot air," i.e., a person prone to exaggeration, boasting, or fibbing like mad.

HOTCHA

A corny yet endearing 1930s expression of delight, usually invoked in an attempt to seem cool. One of the more memorable utterers of this word: a certain Miss Agnes Gooch, frowsy personal secretary to the title character in the book *Auntie Mame* (1955). During one evening out on the town, ol' Agnes has a few too many Pink Whiskers cocktails:

> Agnes slammed her empty glass down and shrieked:
> "Oh, baby, that sets me on fire! Let's have another!" Then, for some
> unaccountable reason, she added: "Hotcha!" . . . The second Pink
> Whiskers arrived and the waiter had hardly set the glass down before
> Agnes had emptied it . . . Then she said "Hotcha!" again.

HOTFOOT

To hurry along. Despite its thirteenth-century origins, the word "hotfoot" was still turning up in the vernaculars of chic young things as late as the 1950s and '60s. For example, the term turns up in Truman Capote's iconic 1958 novella *Breakfast at Tiffany's*. Consult the scene in which indicted glamour girl protagonist Holly Golightly reveals her plans to jump bail and hop on a flight to Brazil: "I'm not hot-footing after Jose, if that's what you suppose . . . It's only: why should I waste a perfectly fine ticket? Already paid for? Besides, I've never been to Brazil."

"I DAMN NEAR BROKE MY CRAZY NECK"

The Memorable Vocabulary and Phraseology of Holden Caulfield

The antihero of J. D. Salinger's 1951 novel *The Catcher in the Rye* supplied a hilarious, ubiquitous vocabulary for several subsequent generations of angst-filled teens. Many of the words and phrases below appear on the book's very first page and occur with indignant regularity.

Corny

Crap / crappy

Crumby

Get a bang out of [insert activity]

Give her the time

Goddam

Horse around

It just about killed me / damn near killed me

Knocked me out

[Old / crappy / phony / interesting / sorry / sad / icy / rusty / pretty / playful] as hell

Phony / phonies

Prince

Lousy with rocks (i.e., jewels) / glasses / perverts

Terrific [liar / friend / dancer / fart]

Terrifically [bored / tired / intelligent / nice]

Touchy as hell

HOTHEAD

A "ginger-snap" (see page 82).

HOTSY-TOTSY

Fine; swell; great: "Everything was hotsy-totsy around here — that is, before the police raid."

HOW-DO-YOU-DO

A commotion or quarrel. Very Laurel and Hardy, who always found themselves in how-do-you-do's and "fine messes."

HUNT-ABOUT

A nosy, meddling gossip.

SEE ALSO "GADABOUT"

HUZZAH

A zippier, old-fashioned alternative to common old celebratory exclamations "hurrah" and "hooray."

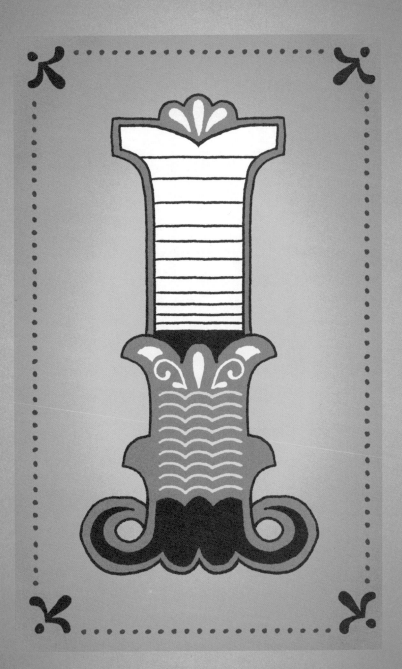

I'LL BE A MONKEY'S UNCLE

An old exclamation expressing utter disbelief: "Old Miss Kneebone is getting married? Well, I'll be a monkey's uncle!" The phrase may allude to Darwinism and the incredulousness that many nineteenth-century people felt about having ancestors in common with the ape at the local zoo.

IN a FAUNCH
[and OTHER GRANDMOTHERLY MIDWESTERNISMS]

Hailing from the American midwest (the previous generations in my family were all born in Illinois), I miss out East, some of the colorful regional locutions that added sweetness, savor and crackle to conversation, in the way that bacon gets a caramelized crispness when you scatter sugar on it as it sizzles (a southern Illinoisan cooking trick). Here are some expressions I miss. From my Great Grandmother Elsie Hartwig: "Well, land's sakes!" (An expression of mild amazement for those who do not like to take the Lord's name in vain.) From my Grandmother Joyce Hupp: "She went into a swivet" (a kind of mini-tantrum, usually applied to women) and "He was in a faunch" (to be in a bad mood—used both of men and women equally).

LIESL SCHILLINGER • LITERARY CRITIC, *THE NEW YORK TIMES BOOK REVIEW*

IN A HUFF

Not happy. In fact, the opposite of happy: peeved.

IN A JIFFY

Quickly. ("Don't worry: I'll have those pigs slopped in a jiffy.")

IN A PICKLE

In an awkward or difficult situation. Even Shakespeare enjoyed the phrase, used here in *The Tempest*:

ALONSO:
How camest thou in this pickle?

TRINCULO:
I have been in such a pickle since I saw you last.

IN A SNIT

Same as "in a huff." Also delightful is the related term "snit-fit": "Oh, don't touch his toy soldier collection; he'll have an absolute snit-fit if you do."

IN CLOVER

Happy.

IN THE FULLNESS of TIME

This biblical term refers to the right, appropriate time for an event to occur—the fitting moment for something to happen that is anticipated but has not yet come to pass (like the coming of the Messiah):

"But when the fullness of time had come, God sent forth his Son... to redeem those who were under the law..." (Galatians 4:4-5, ESV)

My mentor and dear friend, The Reverend Professor Peter J. Gomes, the most elegant person at Harvard for decades, used this term often when encouraging patience and confidence in the belief that something would come to pass as expected... like drinks... or dinner... or the delivery of the first draft of a manuscript to his editor.

LUKE IVES PONTIFELL • FOUNDER AND PUBLISHER, THORNWILLOW PRESS, LTD.

INK-SLINGER

A journalist, author, or other "brother of the quill," according the 1905 *Dictionary of Slang and Colloquial English*.

IRONCLAD

A maddeningly, determinedly chaste girl.

JACK

Money. Let us return once again to children's novel *Harriet the Spy* (see also "fink") for a colorful illustration of the term's use. In the book's pages, a delivery boy ruminates on the bill-paying habits of the wealthy: "They got all that jack and they still don't pay."

fig. 17: IN MY OTHER PANTS

JACK NASTY FACE

A hilarious old seafaring term for "sailor."

JAZZ

A very Liza Minnelli-ish term, who, in the 1970s and '80s, famously crooned out a version of "All That Jazz" from the 1975 musical *Chicago*; throughout the course of the song, she rouges her knees and paints the town and "all that jazz." In this context, it means "something exciting," but under other circumstances, the term was also used to denote "insincere" or windbaggish chat: "Oh, don't give me that jazz about your *yacht* again: it's only a dinghy!"

JEEZ LOUISE

Just who was this Louise person? She likely didn't exist. The "jeez" part of "jeez Louise"—which is sort of a whiny, nasal sigh upon hearing surprising or disappointing news—is derived from "Jesus," and Louise just happens to rhyme with "jeez." And so it goes.

THE JIG IS UP

An Elizabethan phrase, usually meaning that some sort of ruse has been detected and the perpetrator will be brought to justice. The explanation is boringly literal: apparently the word "jig" used to be slang for "a practical joke" or a "witty arch trick," and when the jig was up, your victims were on to you. It's much more interesting to imagine that it meant "the jig (i.e., the dance) is up (over), and it's time to pay the fiddler."

THAT CAT'S GOT CHOPS

Old-Guard Slang from the Realm of Jazz

Just as jazz created a new universe of musical improvisation,
it gave rise to a whole host of verbal expressions as well. What follows
is a short list of some of the more amusing or colorful terms
that you might have heard in the smoky jazz clubs decades ago.

....

Axe An instrument of any variety.

Blow The act of playing any instrument.

Boogie man A critic.

Cat A man who plays jazz.

Chops Good technique ("He's got great chops"), or mouth and
facial muscles needed to play a trumpet or some such.

Clinker A bad note.

Daddy-O One jazz hipster's way of addressing another jazz
hipster.

Gas Something moving or amazing ("That song was a real gas").

Hep / hepcat Someone in the know. As one source puts it,
"[hep] was eventually replaced by 'hip' about the same time that
'cool' replaced 'hot.'"

Hotcha An old-guard exclamation, used to express approval or
delight. Invariably appeared in writing followed by an exclamation point ("Hotcha!"), and was eventually only used by very
corny people.

Hotplate A hot recording, the latest record.

Licks An improvised solo; its player was often said to be "laying
down some hot licks."

JIGGERY-POKERY

Underhanded scheming. ("I shan't tolerate any more of your jiggery-pokery or shenanigans, sir.")

JINGLE-BRAINS

A rattle-brained, "harum-scarum" (see page 92) fellow.

JOHNNY-ON-THE-SPOT

In the old days, a "Johnny-on-the-spot" was a rather earnest person who was on hand to help in any emergency and generally save the day. These days, in New York City, the phrase has received something of a demotion, as it's the name of a company that rents portable toilets.

JOIN THE GYPSIES

An exclamation of exasperation: "If I don't win the church pie-making contest this year, I'm going to run off and join the gypsies!"

JOIN THE MAJORITY

To buy the farm (see page 29).

JUICE

Alcohol. A "juice joint" was a bar or tavern.

SEE ALSO "GIGGLE WATER"

fig. 18: HERE'S TO YOU

KEEN AS MUSTARD

Lavishly enthusiastic—and therefore probably also a tad annoying. The phrase likely references the "keenness"—i.e., intensity and spiciness—of mustard, considered an essential condiment for beef and roasts for centuries.

KEEP YOUR PECKER UP

While this phrase likely sounds distinctly pornographic to modern ears, it was actually quite chaste: when you told a nineteenth-century someone to "keep his pecker up," you were encouraging him to stay cheerful. The "pecker" in question referred not to one's manhood, but rather his nose (think of a bird's beak, or pecker). The phrase is akin to today's wholly unobjectionable "keep your head held high."

KERFUFFLE

This flowery, old-fashioned word for a "commotion" or "disturbance" is particularly amusing when the kerfuffle in question is not particularly flowery.

KETTLE OF FISH

When you landed in this sort of kettle, you were finding yourself amidst a confused state of affairs; a muddle. Imagine being plunked into a vat of wiggling, slippery fish, and you'll understand why this phrase makes perfect sense. Regarding its origin, one source—*The Farlex Trivia Dictionary*—asserts that it was "a corruption of 'kiddle of fish,' in which a kiddle is a basket set in the opening of a weir for catching fish."

KICK THE BUCKET

Die. Also: "kick up the heels."

SEE ALSO "BUY THE FARM" *and* "JOIN THE MAJORITY"

KICKSY-WICKSY

Restless. Not to be confused with plain old "kicksy," which meant "disagreeable" and "troublesome."

KIDDO

A grand old agent here at ICM—who represented *Gone with the Wind*—used to call me "kiddo." She was 90 at the time. And when she left she told me, "You're a great dame."

ESTHER NEWBERG • LEGENDARY LITERARY AGENT

KIDDYISH

Sounds like an old-guard synonym for "jejune" or "immature," but it actually means "modish" or "up-to-date." ("Check out the kiddyish handlebar moustache on that guy.")

KILLING

An adjective meaning "bewitching; alluring; beguiling." Because of the murderous connotations associated with the word's primary definition, one imagines that sexy, mysterious *film noir* dames would fall into the "killing" category.

KISSER

Mouth. This mid-century slang word was immortalized by Jackie Gleason's Ralph on the 1950s TV series *The Honeymooners*, who regularly blusters to his wife: "One of these days, Alice—*pow*! Right in the kisser." Luckily, the sharp-tongued Alice gave as good as she got, and her kisser remained unscathed.

KNEE-HIGH TO A MOSQUITO

A nasty little expression once used to describe a person of little significance; a nobody.

KNEES-UP

A boisterous dance party: "There's quite a knees-up going on over at the roadhouse tonight." Likely derived from the early twentieth-century music hall song "Knees Up Mother Brown":

> *Oh, knees up Mother Brown,*
> *Knees up Mother Brown,*
> *Come along, dearie, let it go*
> *E-I-E-I-E-I-Oh!*
> *It's your blooming birthday*
> *Let's wake up all the town;*
> *So knees up, knees up*
> *Don't get the breeze up*
> *Knees up Mother Brown!*

KNIFISH

An appropriately sharp old word for "spiteful."

KNOCKABOUT MAN

A jack-of-all-trades, i.e., a person who does many different sorts of work. It makes perfect sense to revive this phrase today, when so many people have to hold down a plethora of jobs to make ends meet.

KNOCK AROUND

To fool or mess around.

KNOCK ME OVER WITH A FEATHER

An exclamation of extreme astonishment: "When I found out that she was really a 'he,' you could have knocked me over with a feather."

KNOCK SOMEONE'S SOCKS OFF

To surprise or impress the hell out of someone.

KNOCKER-FACE

An unsightly person.

KNUCKLE SANDWICH

A punch in the mouth with a closed fist. Otherwise known as a "bunch-of-fives" (page 28) in action.

fig. 19: WHY I OUGHTTA...

KOOKY

While "kooky" has been defined as "odd, cranky, or crazy," the old word is actually far more specific than that. A kooky person is indeed peculiar, but innocuously so. Each of us knows a true kook, usually the owner of the local arts and crafts store, the old lady in apartment 8C who wears rubber boots and tiaras every day, and so on.

LA-DE-DAH

This silly little phrase is great both as an exclamation ("She moved to the Upper East Side? Well, la-de-dah!") and as an adjective ("I refuse to go to Swifty's for lunch again: it's far too hoity-toity and la-de-dah.")

LAMB AND SALAD

In the old days, if you gave someone "lamb and salad," you weren't actually serving him a lovely dinner. Quite the contrary: you were, in fact, giving him a sound "batty-fanging" (see page 18).

LAP-FUL

Nineteenth-century slang for "lover."

LATCH-PAN

The lower lip. Best used in the following old phrase: "hang one's latch-pan," or sulk. ("If you keep hanging your ol' latch-pan like that, it's going to stay that way forever—and then you'll *really* have something to sulk about.")

LAUGH IN ONE'S SLEEVE

When you laugh in (or up) your own sleeve, you are, in fact, snickering quietly to yourself while maintaining a façade of gravity. Usually you would be doing this as some fool in your proximity was presenting a "harebrained" (see page 92) scheme, idea, or just generally blustering away.

LAY DOWN THE FORK AND KNIFE

To depart from this world.

SEE ALSO "JOIN THE MAJORITY"

OLDSPEAK

*Literary Works
That Introduced Famous Fictional Languages*

••• In George Orwell's *1984*, the totalitarian regime imposes a language known as "Newspeak" on its oppressed subjects. Rebellious thoughts–or "thoughtcrime"–are the target of this vernacular, which shrinks and hardens the English language (known as "Oldspeak") down to a joyless nub. To illustrate: the Newspeak translation of the entire introduction to the Declaration of Independence is distilled down to one word–"crimethink."

••• Richard Adams's *Watership Down* treated readers to the language of "Lapine," derived from the Latin word for rabbit (*lapin*) and used by the novel's fictional rabbit characters. The non-rabbit characters in the book speak a language known as "hedgerow."

••• J. R. R. Tolkien's *Lord of the Rings* works feature a slew of languages spoken by the inhabitants of his Middle-earth. For his fictional Elves alone, Tolkien constructed the grammar and vocabulary of at least fifteen Elvish languages and dialects, including "Primitive Quendian," "Common Eldarin," "Quenya," "Goldogrin," "Telerin," and "Avarin."

••• *A Clockwork Orange* by Anthony Burgess–showcasing another rather grim dystopian society–introduced "Nadsat," a vernacular spoken by the antihero teenagers in the books. Burgess–a linguist as well as a novelist–meticulously crafted the language as a Russian-influenced version of English.

LAZY-MAN'S LOAD

More than one can carry. At first glance, this seems counterintuitive; after all, wouldn't a lazy man want to carry *less* than his share? But coiners of the term were looking at it from a different angle: lazy men will carry more than they can handle in the first trip, to avoid making a second trip.

LEAD ON A MERRY CHASE

To give someone the "runaround," "beat around the bush," "pussyfoot," or "waffle." In other words, to lead someone on a pointless venture.

LEAD SOMEONE DOWN THE GARDEN PATH

To mislead someone. One early, spirited example of the phrase comes to us courtesy of Ethel Mannin's 1926 book about the advertising business, *Sounding Brass,* in which one character blurts out: "They're cheats, that's wot women are! Lead you up the garden path and then go snivellin' around 'cos wot's natcheral."

Another great, similar old saying: "lead one to a pretty dance," or cause someone unnecessary trouble.

LEAVE WELL ENOUGH ALONE

Few of us can resist the urge to tweak. But this old saying reminds us that sometimes further "improvements" or further interference will actually make things worse, and that we should leave what's been done "well enough" alone. An illustrative excerpt from a story in *The Ghosts of Nantucket* (1984) by Blue Balliett: "We didn't shine a light into the room out of some feeling, I suppose, that we had already disturbed the presence, whatever it was, and that we should leave well enough alone."

LEFT-HANDED COMPLIMENT

Old-guard alternative for "backhanded compliment," or a bit of flattery that, in reality, insults its recipient. In the past, the "left" was considered unlucky or undesirable: for example, the saying "get up on the wrong side of the bed" (see page 82) was also often invoked as "left side of the bed"—and people used to take great pains to heave themselves out on the right side each morning. Also, a "left-handed oath" was considered nonbinding.

LEG-BAIL

To escape, beat it out of town.

LICKSPITTLE

A seventeenth-century term for a lowly sort of parasitical cretin who tolerates all sorts of indignities for the sake of certain advantages. A first cousin to the "flunky" (see page 74).

LILY-LIVERED

Cowardly. Used frequently by Old Hollywood's bowlegged cowboys and spats-wearing, cigar-chomping gangsters: "Why you low-down, lily-livered, chicken-hearted worm—you call yourself a man?" But the phrase was also used in more elite realms, such as Shakespeare's *Macbeth*:

> MACBETH (to Servant):
> Go prick thy face and over-red thy fear.
> You lily-livered boy . . .
> Those linen cheeks of thine
> Are counsellers to fear.

LIP-CLAP

Sixteenth-century slang for "a kiss." Another variation: "lip-favour," and the act of kissing was called "lip-labour."

LOBLOLLY

A seventeenth-century oaf or a lout. A similar-sounding synonym from the same time period: "looby." Also consider resurrecting the slightly older word "lobcock"—i.e., a "blockhead" or "dunce."

LOCOMOTIVE

Instead of train. It just sounds more romantic.

SEE ALSO "MOTOR"

fig. 20: ALL ABOARD

LOLLPOOP

A lazy idler.

LOLLYGAG

To dawdle, hang around. A perfect word for parents with lazy offspring: "Why don't you spend some time outdoors instead of lollygagging around the mall all the time? You're turning green for lack of sunlight."

LONG DRINK OF WATER

Also sometimes uttered as "tall glass of water," this phrase is used to describe a toothsome, gorgeous, desire-provoking woman. Anyone who's ever had an urgent thirst will relate to the voluptuous relief that comes with getting your mitts on a tall glass of cold water; one imagines the same enjoyment coming from firkytoodling (see page 72) with a great-looking dame.

LONG IN THE TOOTH

Old. Horses' teeth continue to grow as they age; hence this saying, which came into popularity in the nineteenth century. Playwright Noël Coward later conjured it up fairly regularly, as evidenced by this impish 1963 entry in his personal diary:

> On Sunday night we went to Martha Graham's opening night. Company brilliantly disciplined but, oh dear! I know she is a great genius and the foremost innovator of modern ballet . . . but she really is a bit long in the tooth now to go running about the stage on her knees, and even when she was young it wasn't a very sensible thing to do.

LONG-HEADED

At first glance, this sounds like an insult; after all, who would welcome the insinuation that they have an oblong head? But in the eighteenth century, it was something of a compliment, meaning "far-sighted," "clever," and "shrewd."

LOOPY

Kooky (see page 113).

LOSE ONE'S MARBLES

A gentle, old-guard way to say "go crazy." ("Mrs. Beeswax must have lost her marbles: she started making Jell-O molds a week ago and hasn't stopped for a second.")

LOST BALL IN THE HIGH WEEDS

Someone who has no idea what the hell he or she is doing.

LOOSE LADIES

Old Words for Women of Ill-Repute

The quaintness of some of these terms
often makes them seem more redemptive than damning.

Barber's chair	Hussy
Dolly-mop	Ladybird
Drab	Mutton
Fad-cattle	Slattern
Floozy	Strumpet
Fusty luggs	Tart
Harlot	Tramp
Harpy	Trollop

LOUSE

This word should be brought back as a noun ("That louse ran off and stuck me with the rent and all of the bills—not to mention *fleas*"), a verb ("I *knew* that she would louse up that paint job; the whole kitchen looks like a Jackson Pollock painting"), and an adjective ("I don't know why he bothers wearing that lousy eye patch—it keeps falling off, and anyway, he has two perfectly good eyes").

LOVE-LADDER

A rascally old slang term for "lace petticoat." It could easily be revived today and applied to lace stockings.

LUG

There really seems to be no limit to the number of insulting "L" words when it comes to describing men. "Lug" means "a stupid or awkward man"; in the old days, it was usually squawked when said lug had unwittingly affronted feminine sensibilities: "You big lug! You spilled coffee all over my new shoes!"

LULU

This pleasing, roll-off-the-tongue word has had various connotations: on one hand, in the nineteenth century, it was invoked to describe a beautiful woman; a knockout. It later became a synonym for "humdinger" as well: "a lulu of a black eye," "a lulu of an oil spill," "a lulu of a fight." Either way, it's revival-worthy.

LUMP IT

As in, "You can like it or lump it." Perfect for harried mothers, bosses, and teachers who are weary of tolerating whiners.

LUMPSHIOUS

An unlikely old word for "delicious."

LUNCHEON

"Lunch" is something you grab. "Luncheon" is a civilized experience. The full word was a casualty of America's ongoing love affair with brutish abbreviation.

MADCAP

A now-underused word meaning "wildly or heedlessly impulsive; reckless; rash"; often used in conjunction with "follies," "hijinks," or "antics." *Très* 1920s.

MAKE BRICKS WITHOUT STRAW

To labor away at something without having the necessary materials to do the job adequately. A counterpoint to the Pollyanna-ish old phrase, "When life gives you lemons, make lemonade."

MAKE TRACKS

To hightail it; beat it; scramble someplace in a hurry. Refers to the tracks—or footprints—left behind in your wake.

SEE ALSO "LEG-BAIL"

MAKE WHOOPEE

Today's dictionaries are surprisingly prissy when it comes to defining "making whoopee" (sometimes written as "whoopie," but "whoopee" is more old-fashioned): these sources assert that the term meant "to revel," "make merry," or "celebrate noisily." But as many people still likely know, the term used to describe the sort of amorous activity usually reserved for beds and backseats. The act itself was, of course, great fun, but jazz and blues musicians took care to note that the results were usually less romantic:

He's washin' dishes and baby clothes . . .
That's what you get folks, for makin' whoopee

"MAKIN' WHOOPEE" (1928) *by* WALTER DONALDSON AND GUS KAHN

SEE ALSO "FIRKYTOODLE"

"TO ERR IS HUMAN, BUT IT FEELS DIVINE"

The Sassy One–Liners of Old Hollywood Actress Mae West

So sassy, in fact, that the bawdy Ms. West was banned from NBC Radio after a scandalous, double entendre–laden guest appearance in 1937. All of her once universally famous quips are preservation-worthy:

· ·

"I used to be Snow White, but I drifted."

"Too much of a good thing can be wonderful."

"A hard man is good to find."

"When I'm good, I'm very good – but when I'm bad, I'm better."

"Good girls go to heaven. Bad girls go everywhere else."

"When women go wrong, men go right after them."

· ·

MARRIAGE-MUSIC

And while we're on the topic of the aftereffects of whoopee-making, let us consider the seventeenth-century term "marriage-music," i.e., the crying of babies and children.

MARVELOUS

Whereas today we might drag out the syllables of the word "ammmaaaaazzzz-ing" to describe something that we find wonderful or delightful, "marvelous" was the go-to description among the chicly appreciative in the 1950s and '60s. Consider the following famous exclamation from the 1957 film *Funny Face*, in which Audrey Hepburn—playing a bookish gamine—resists the efforts of a pushy fashion editor to give her a makeover: "Stop! I don't want my hair cut! I don't want my eyebrows up or down. I want them right where they are! And I see no functional advantage in a marvelous mouth."

MASHER

As one British etymologist puts it, "a man who thought himself irresistible to the female sex but whose advances were often unwelcome." The word may have gone, but the need for it clearly has not.

MEALY-MOUTHED

Timid. Although the word was all the rage circa 1572, it was still turning up as an insult centuries later. As Scarlett O'Hara said about her rival Melanie Wilkes in the 1939 film *Gone with the Wind*: "She's a pale-faced, mealy-mouthed ninny, and I hate her."

MELLOW

A 1970s term for "chilled-out" or "relaxed." The award for creepiest use of the word goes to Paul Simon in his role as sleazy film producer Tony Lacey in the 1977 film *Annie Hall*: "We're going back to the Pierre [Hotel], and we're gonna meet Jack and Anjelica . . . if you'd like to come, we'd love to have you. We could just sit and talk, [and] just be very mellow." (The "Jack" and "Anjelica" in question, were, of course Jack Nicholson and Anjelica Huston, making Lacey a name-dropper as well as a sleaze.)

MELTING BUTTER IN A WIG

A laugh-out-loud funny old phrase meaning "ridiculousness" or "nonsense."

MEMENTO MORI

I think that death should play a bigger role in our lives. Socrates taught that we should "practice death" daily to help us remember what's really important. And the ancient Romans used to carve "MM" on the bases of statues and the trunks of trees. The letters stand for Memento Mori—"Remember Death." This wasn't a sign of morbidity, but a way to bring perspective into our lives and a mental tool with which to overcome our fear of the unknown and come to terms with life's only inevitability. Bringing back this phrase can help us appreciate life to the fullest.

ARIANNA HUFFINGTON • PRESIDENT AND EDITOR-IN-CHIEF, THE HUFFINGTON POST MEDIA GROUP; AUTHOR

MILKSOP

Another one of those innocuous-sounding yet utterly cutting words, "milksop" was fourteenth-century slang for "a weak or ineffectual person." A synonym: "milquetoast." Both refer to the bland culinary dish of milk toast: a dish of bread soaked in warm milk, dished up for fussy infants and invalids. Another variation: "milk-and-water," which was variously used as an adjective and a noun.

MIND YOUR OWN BEESWAX

Meaning: "mind your own damn business." There are several theories about the saying's origin. Among the most colorful: In the nineteenth century, women used beeswax-based makeup on their faces to smooth the skin. If they sat too close to the hearth fire, the wax would start to melt. If a woman was caught staring at another's melting makeup, she would be told to "mind your own beeswax." True? Who knows. Amusing? Definitely.

MINGY

I've always loved *mingy*, a word that's so neglected that it doesn't even show up in my *Webster's*, Second Edition. And it's fairly recent in origin, too: late nineteenth century. It's listed as meaning stingy, mean, or niggardly, but I love the way it has an associative pathos to it, as well: I always think, when I hear it, of a little domestic arrangement that's unutterably sad in its implacable poverty but still viewed with compassion. Some particularly affecting corner of the Cratchits' home, for example.

JIM SHEPARD • AUTHOR OF *YOU THINK THAT'S BAD*, *PROJECT X*, AND *LIKE YOU'D UNDERSTAND, ANYWAY*

MISS NANCY

A prim person who's absolutely lousy with affectations.

SEE ALSO "GOODY-GOODY"

MOLLYCODDLE

A boy or man who's used to being pampered, coddled, and indulged. Also divine as a verb: "That kid is going to be a total nightmare if his mother keeps mollycoddling him like that."

SEE ALSO "BRAT"

MONKEY AROUND

To mess around, get up to no good. In other words, behave like a mischievous, curious, impish little monkey.

SEE ALSO "HORSE AROUND"

MONKEY WITH A LONG TAIL

A mortgage.

MOOCHER

A person who borrows with no intention of repayment. It's quite an old word, possibly stemming from the Middle English "mucchen," which meant to hoard or to be stingy, or even "to keep coins in one's nightcap," according to etymologist Douglas Harper.

MOONRAKE

To idle.

SEE ALSO "GATHER WOOL"

COLD HARD CASH

Terms for "Money" Over the Centuries

Over the years, everyone seems to have used a different slang word
for "money." One thing that all generations could likely agree on:
there's never been enough of it, then or now.

Ace	Dough
Bacon	Fin
Ballast	Gingerbread
Bank	Gravy
Beans	Greenbacks
Bones	Horse-nails
Boodle	Jack
Booty	Lettuce
Bread	Long green
Cabbage	Moolah
Chicken feed	Scratch
Chinkers	Spondulicks
Clams	Rhino
Coal	
Coin	
Coppers	
Corks	
Doubloon	

MOONSHINY

Unreal; ephemeral.

MOPSY

A slovenly, dowdy, or generally unappealing woman.

SEE ALSO "SLATTERN"

MOREISH

Another vintage word for which there has been no adequate replacement, "moreish" means "causing the desire for more" and is usually used in reference to food. *The Dictionary of Slang and Colloquial English* (1905) sums up the term best: "When there is scarcely enough of an eatable or drinkable, it is said to taste moreish." This term could be revived to describe red velvet cake in any quantity.

SEE ALSO "ALL-OVERISH"

MOSSYBACK

An irredeemably old-fashioned person.

MOTOR

As in, "Why don't we motor out to the countryside for a picnic?"

MUBBLEFUBBLES

Low spirits. Perhaps akin to Holly Golightly's "mean reds."

MUCH ADO ABOUT NOTHING

A phrase most frequently associated with Shakespeare, of course, who penned a play by this title circa 1599. The meaning: a big fuss over a matter of little or no importance. Wildly applicable to more than half of the "kerfuffles" (see page 109) that take place in contemporary office culture, and therefore infinitely bring-back-worthy.

SEE ALSO "NOTHING TO WRITE HOME ABOUT"

MUCKRAKE

The journalistic act of hunting for and publishing scandalous information about public figures, a process often likened to raking through "muck" and dirt. Some sources credit President Theodore Roosevelt with the word's popularization; he used it while presiding over the country at a time during which newspapers were printing increasingly sensationalist headlines and sordid, not-always-true exposés. It's perhaps as—if not more—applicable now, in the age of invasive, "gotcha" Internet journalism, as it was in the early 1900s epoch of "yellow journalism."

MULE IN A HORSE'S HARNESS

A rather damning idiom describing rabble-like, ostentatious people who're acting above their station, or decked out in the adornments of a superior class. This could easily describe half of the creatures who appear on today's reality television shows.

MUNDUNGUS

Stinking; fetid-smelling. ("If you don't get those mundungus sneakers out of here, I'm going to toss them into a bonfire in the backyard.")

MUSN'T-MENTION-'EMS

Intimate garments.

SEE ALSO "LOVE-LADDER"

NACKY

Old slang for "ingenious," or "full of knacks."

NAGGLE

To toss one's head in a terribly affected manner. Since such head-tossing of this variety hasn't gone out of style (and likely never will), this old term shouldn't have, either.

NAIL LACQUER

Because what we call "nail polish" today is not polish. It is lacquer.

NAMBY-PAMBY

To flatter someone: "She namby-pambied the butcher into giving her a free turkey." As an adjective, it has also been used to describe an insipid or indecisive person.

NAUGHTY-PACK

A half-disdaining, half-affectionate old term for "children."

SEE ALSO "MARRIAGE-MUSIC"

NEAT AS A PIN

A pleasing phrase meaning "tidy and orderly." One source claims that the phrase originated in the early nineteenth century, when mass production began to ensure a certain uniformity of products—presumably including pins, which beforehand would have been handmade and likely uneven.

NEAT-O

A quaint, kindergarten-ish synonym for "cool." ("Wow, your pilgrim diorama is really neat-o!")

NECK

A contribution from the 1950s, "necking" meant to make out or "firkytoodle" (see page 72). Necking sessions usually took place in the backseat of a car (an act which itself was called "parking"), preferably at a drive-in movie theater (which was known as a "passion pit").

NE'ER-DO-WELL

Eighteenth-century slang for an idler, loafer, or "vile wastrel." One old dictionary's summation: "A person of confirmed bad habits." Our modern version is, of course, a "good-for-nothing."

NEGGLEDIGEE

Bumpkinish slang for "negligee."

NERVOUS NELLIE

A 1920s term for an unduly, annoyingly nervous person. "Nervous Nellie" probably didn't refer to an actual person, but was likely a product of that era's affection for alliteration. Plus, it was used to describe both women *and* men, and presumably calling a man by a woman's name added insult to injury. Perhaps ol' Nellie was a second cousin to "Miss Nancy" (see page 129).

NIFFY-NAFFY

Quavery-wavery (see page 165).

NIFTY

An amiable adjective with a variety of positive connotations: "smart or stylish," "excellent or fine," "sizeable." All three of these definitions likely apply in the following excerpt:

> Next to [Charlotte], attached to the ceiling, Wilbur saw
> a curious object. It was a sort of sac, or cocoon. It was peach-colored
> and looked as though it were made of cotton candy.
>
> "What is that nifty thing? Did you make it?" [Wilbur asked.]
> "Is it a plaything?"
>
> "Plaything?" [replied Charlotte.] "I should say not.
> It is my egg sac, my magnum opus."

—E.B. White, *Charlotte's Web* (1952)

NINCOMPOOP

A simpleton or fool; falls into the fun-to-say category. Some have ventured to assert that the seventeenth-century term is a compression of the Latin phrase *non compos mentis* ("mentally incompetent"); yet other etymologists believe that it was likely a bastardization of a proper name.

SEE ALSO "LOLLPOOP"

NINE-DAYS'-WONDER

Anything that causes a great deal excitement, which then fizzles away and is heard of no more:

> KING EDWARD IV:
> You'll think it strange if I should marry her.
>
> GLOUCESTER:
> That would be ten days' wonder at the least.
>
> CLARENCE:
> That's a day longer than a wonder lasts.

—William Shakespeare, *King Henry VI*

NINNYHAMMER

A twin term to "nincompoop" (see page 137), the equally pleasing "nin-nyhammer" also described a "foolish, incompetent person." It was often shortened to plain old "ninny" for those too lazy to utter the entire phrase.

SEE ALSO "MEALY-MOUTHED"

NIPPER

A pickpocket: "That young nipper just made off with my moustache wax! However will I last until I can buy a new tin?" Also written as "nypper," "nabber," or "nabbler." A great synonym from around the same time period: "cut-purse."

NITWIT

Part of the "nincompoop" and "ninnyhammer" clan, which appears to be having something of a family reunion in this section. "Nitwit," which signifies a "slow-witted" person, was often shortened to "nit," and usually wielded in sentences like this: "Don't listen to a word she says; after all, she's just a silly little nit.")

NO-COUNT

As a noun: a "ne'er-do-well" (see page 136), and as an adjective, "a sorry excuse," "without merit." A variation of the term was memorably used in the old song "You're Just a No Account," crooned out variously by Billie Holiday, Louis Armstrong, and other notable blues and jazz singers: throughout the course of the song, the "No Account" in question will never amount "to nothing at all."

NO DICE

Meaning "nothing doing" or "no deal." Most sources agree that it is an early twentieth-century American phrase from the gambling realm, but disagree about the exact origin. One source posits the theory that the phrase has to do with dice-throwing games like craps, in which an invalid throw (when a throw is out of play or a die isn't lying flat) is ruled as "no-dice." But another insists that the phrase stems from an era when dice games were illegal in many states, and gamblers hid dice from police during raids. According to etymologist Gary Martin, "Courts would sometimes throw out cases if the dice weren't offered in evidence . . . It is very likely that the 'no dice, no conviction' ruling is the source of the current meaning of 'no dice.'"

NOBBY

A fashionable or chic person in the late eighteenth and early nineteenth centuries might have been described as "nobby." ("That's quite a nobby dress and hat you have there—surely they must have come all the way from Poiret in Paris!")

NODDLE-CASE

A wig. "Noddle" was a late sixteenth-century word for "head."

SEE ALSO "WIGANOWNS"

NOGOODNIK

A "no-count" or "ne'er-do-well." This 1940s term for "a worthless person" may have come from a Yiddish interpretation of the Russian word *негодник* (nye-GOD-nik).

NON-CON

"A nonconformist, Presbyterian, or any other dissenter." Colorful definition courtesy of *Grose's Classical Dictionary of the Vulgar Tongue* (1823).

NONE OF YOUR AFFAIR

An airy old way of saying, "That's none of your business."

SEE ALSO "MIND YOUR OWN BEESWAX"

NOSY PARKER

A busybody; a prying person—primarily a British slang phrase. Some believe that the "Parker" in question was Matthew Parker, a sixteenth-century archbishop of Canterbury, who apparently ordered some intrusive and unpopular inquiries into the private lives of the clergy. He also reportedly had a rather large nose.

However, the phrase didn't really start appearing in print until the late 1800s, leaving etymologists to conclude that it had different origins. One of them—Hugh Rawson, author of *Wicked Words* (1989)—points out that, in the late nineteenth century, the word "parker" alluded to a park keeper, and concludes that the earliest "nosy parkers" were likely creeps who slunk around public parks, spying on "firkytoodling" (see page 72) couples. Adds *The Word Detective*: "It strikes me that, in that pre-automotive age, jokes involving 'nosy parkers' were probably as common as our modern 'cop on Lovers Lane' variety was in the 1950s."

SEE ALSO "GADABOUT" *and* "QUIZ"

NOT A FEATHER TO FLY WITH

Impoverished; ruined. ("Bernie Madoff didn't leave many of his clients a feather to fly with.")

SEE ALSO "COOK ONE'S GOOSE" *and* "CURTAINS"

NOTHING TO WRITE HOME ABOUT

I.e., nothing special. Such a grandmotherly turn of phrase, yet *so* withering.

NOW YOU'RE ON THE TROLLEY

Meaning, "*Now* you've caught on." There is an implied "finally" tacked on to the end of that sentence.

SEE ALSO "GET THE DRIFT"

NUDGE

A nag or a tedious person. This word was often invoked by comedian Carol Burnett in her 1970s variety television show, *The Carol Burnett Show*; she made nudges into a regular comic presence. Go online and find videos of her sketches "No Frills Airplane" and "Hospital Nudge" to see nudgery at its best.

NUTS TO YOU

The opposite of "bouquets to you" (see page 26).

ODD-COME-SHORTLY'S

In the olden days, when you said "I'll get around to it one of these odd-come-shortly's," you meant that you'd attempt said task one of these days. A peculiar expression, but pleasing nonetheless.

OFF ONE'S NUT

Mad as a hatter. Also: "off one's rocker" and "off one's chump."

OGLES

Eyes.

THE OLD ADAM

An old phrase with clear biblical roots, meaning man's supposed natural tendency toward sin and general naughtiness. ("Well, I never! He ate that entire pie, didn't leave a scrap for anyone else, and then blamed the old Adam in him.")

OLD HEAD ON YOUNG SHOULDERS

A term describing someone who is wise beyond one's years.

OLD MR. GRIM

Death.

OLD-TIMER

A person of advanced years.

OLD SPLIT-FOOT

A Curiously Aged Devil

For whatever reason, in bygone times, Lucifer was assigned a wide array of nicknames that began with "old," including the following:

Old Bendy	Old Poger
Old Blazes	Old Poker
Old Driver	Old Roger
Old Gooseberry	Old Scratch
Old Harry	Old Toast
Old Nick	
Old One (or Old 'Un)	

ON A TEAR

I.e., on a bender; an extended, boozy carouse. Used facetiously in the 1935 Marx Brothers film *A Night at the Opera*. Groucho and Chico are negotiating a contract and resolving contested clauses by ripping them out of the contract. At one point, Chico notices that their respective shredded contracts are of different lengths, and asks, "Hey—how is it that my contract is skinnier than yours?" Replies Groucho: "Well, I dunno. You must have been out on a tear last night."

ON A TOOT

On a tear. Except more fun, from the sound of it.

ON PINS AND NEEDLES

Nervous; uncomfortable. As you would expect of someone perched atop a bunch of pins and needles.

ON THE BLINK

Broken.

ON THE MUSCLE

Looking for a fight.

ONE-HORSE

Insignificant or third rate. Usually heard as part of the phrase "one-horse town," i.e., a small, backwater place. The expression obviously references a village too small to have more than one resident horse. It's unclear whether donkeys were factored into the etymological equation.

ONE-TRICK PONY

A person who has only one apparent talent or skill set, or someone who meets with success only once in his life.

OUT AT HEELS

Someone who's fallen on hard times was once said to be "out at heels" or "out at elbows"—perhaps a reference to the worn-down state of the clothing covering those respective areas.

OUT OF COLLAR

Unemployed, and therefore unobliged to wear a collar (or collared shirt) during the day.

SEE ALSO "PAPER-COLLAR"

OUTTA SIGHT

"Neat-o," "groovy," or "dynamite."

OWL-LIGHT

A sweet term for "dusk." However, one who "walked by owl-light" was said to be evading arrest.

OYSTER

Beyond being an aphrodisiac mollusk, in the 1800s, an oyster was also "a jolly good guy." Before *that*, however, it meant a gob of phlegm.

ONCE BITTEN, TWICE SHY

Wise Proverbs Worth Preserving

The proverb often feel like a cousin to the cliché—
but in many instances, old proverbs still ring true and we should
continue to pass them along to the next generations. For instance,
who can argue against the wisdom of the following?

....

A chain is only as strong as its weakest link.

A fool and his money are soon parted.

Don't put all your eggs in one basket.

Birds of a feather flock together.

You can't get blood from a stone.

You catch more flies with honey than with vinegar.

Empty vessels make the most noise.

Handsome is as handsome does.

People who live in glass houses shouldn't throw stones.

You can't make a silk purse from a sow's ear.

He who pays the piper chooses the tune.

P'S AND Q'S

If someone instructed you to "mind your p's and q's," you were being told to mind your manners and be on your best behavior. There are a variety of theories about the phrase's origin: firstly, that p's and q's look similar and therefore schoolmistresses would chide their students to "mind" them and not mix them up. A more delightful explanation: that French dance instructors (or "dancemasters") in bygone eras would admonish their students to mind their *pieds* (feet) and *queues* (wigs) when bowing.

PACK CARDS

To cheat.

PAINT A PICTURE

This old expression was usually conjured up when its exasperated utterer was attempting to explain a situation to a dimwit: "Do you need me to paint you a picture, or what?"

SEE ALSO "GET THE DRIFT" *and* "NOW YOU'RE ON THE TROLLEY"

PANTYWAIST

A "quavery-wavery" (see page 165) or "niffy-naffy" (see page 136) person.

SEE ALSO "MILKSOP"

PAPER-COLLAR

Slang for a well-off man, often used in the nineteenth century. This may sound counter-intuitive—why would a wealthy man affix a paper collar to his shirt every morning? But a variety of sources tell us that paper collars used to be a regular adornment in the dressing rooms of the elite, and even became something of an art form. Says *Knight's American Mechanical Dictionary: A Description of Tools, Instruments, Machines, Processes, and Engineering* (1881), "Collars were occasionally made out of paper, . . . as by Lord Byron, who affected a collar of peculiar shape, somewhat on the sailor pattern." As paper-collar manufacturing advanced, collars were created to resemble linen "with the necessary rigidity and embossing," and even "in imitation of lace." Clearly the coveted adornments of "dandies" (see "dandiprat," page 51), "bit-of-stuffs" (see page 23), and "sparks" (see page 186).

PAPER MARRIAGE

Nineteenth-century slang for "a society wedding" (i.e., a lot of banknotes are changing hands). Reminiscent of the old saying "Money marries money and makes more money."

PARLEYVOO

To speak French—an old humorous respelling of *parlez-vous*.

PATSY

Early 1900s slang for "scapegoat" or "fall guy." It also indicates an easily deceived or swindled person: a "dupe," "chump," or "sap."

PAW PAW

Naughty; impish. For example, "paw paw words" were of the variety never spoken in "polite society" (see page 160) or near "the quality" (see page 164).

PAY THE DEBT OF NATURE

To die.

PEBBLY-BEACHED

Destitute; i.e., "stone" cold broke. Formerly common phrases using this term include "to wash up on the pebbly beach" or "to sight the pebbly beach." There was also the more literal "penniless beach."

PEDDLE YOUR FISH IN THE WRONG MARKET

An entertaining animal-world alternative to the equally old-fashioned "bark up the wrong tree" (see page 17).

PEEL EGGS

To stand on ceremony.

PEEPERS

Sometimes used as a synonym for "spectacles," and at others times used instead of "eyes."

SEE ALSO "BARNACLES"

PENNY DREADFULS

A term for old tabloid-y penny publications, which were filled with all sorts of "dreadful" scandals, exposés, and other sensationalist bits and bobs. Perhaps the term could be updated to "four-dollar dreadfuls" to describe the various scandal mags festooning supermarket checkout counters today.

PENNY SILVER

Someone who thinks that his penny is silver has a rather lofty opinion of himself.

PEPPER IN THE NOSE

To be annoyed or irritated.

PEPPY

The emergence of the now-underused words "pep" and "peppy" predated
the advent of morning television anchors by decades, but might have been
tailor-made for them: each denotes a highly particular sort of "liveliness,"
"bubbly-ness," and "perkiness." Also resurrection-worthy: the phrase "pep
in your step" (as in, "Here, drink this quintuple espresso. *That* will put a
little pep in your step").

PERSNICKETY

It's very fun to say, although its contemporary synonyms are as well:
"nitpicky," "fussy," and "finicky."

PETTISH

A sixteenth-century synonym for the equally wonderful word "peevish."
In fact, standard thesaurus entries for "pettish" list all sorts of divine old-
guard synonyms, including "churlish," "snappish," and "cross."

SEE ALSO "VIXENLY"

PHIZ-GIG

An outlandishly attired woman of mature years. Or, as *The Dictionary of
Slang and Colloquial English* (1905) puts it, "An old ewe dressed lamb-fashion."

PHOOEY

An exclamation of disgust or frustration; a charming, mild utterance compared to its modern counterparts. The word was also used by our grandmothers in contexts like this: "*You* were the one who bought all of the market's canned pumpkin right before Thanksgiving? Well, phooey on you!"

SEE ALSO "NUTS TO YOU"

PI, PIED, PIEING — AS IN PIED TYPE

To throw into disarray. To disarrange. To cause chaos from order. A printer's term from the time of hot metal typography when each letter was an individual piece of cast metal arranged, or set, in blocks of type that would be inked and printed letterpress onto paper. If a galley of type (a long tray of set type) were dropped, you'd have a big unsorted heap of loose, random letters. When you drop organized type, you've pied your type. You've made a big mess of things. So, when you've let a situation get out of control and made a mess of things, that the situation is **pied**. Unlike spilt milk, it *is* something to cry over.

LUKE IVES PONTIFELL • FOUNDER AND PUBLISHER, THORNWILLOW PRESS, LTD.

PICK A HOLE IN A MAN'S COAT

To find fault with someone, or find his weak points.

PICTURE

My grandmother, Frances Spielman, worked in the film business for fifty years and taught me to love the word "picture." The way she said it made movies sound like grand fun, far from the sterile and stern domain of "film." Among her favorite pictures that she worked on and taught me to love: *Room at the Top*, *The Man Who Fell to Earth*, and *Monty Python and the Holy Grail*. I hope you will play hooky one day and spend the afternoon at the cinema watching pictures . . .

GAYLE TZEMACH LEMMON • JOURNALIST;
AUTHOR, *THE DRESSMAKER OF KHAIR KHANA*

PIE IN THE SKY

There are slight variations in definitions given for this phrase. In some cases, it was invoked to describe an unrealistically optimistic goal ("He says that he aims to swim to China, but that's pie in the sky, if you ask me"). In others, "pie in the sky" had somewhat more religious connotations and was used to describe one's heavenly reward. Both definitions are in keeping with the expression's origin, which is frequently attributed to the 1911 song "The Preacher and the Slave" by Joe Hill, a Swedish-born immigrant to the United States who became involved in labor politics. In the song, Hill ridicules preachers who spend their energy "saving souls" instead of feeding the hungry:

> Long-haired preachers come out every night,
> Try to tell you what's wrong and what's right;
> But when asked how 'bout something to eat
> They will answer with voices so sweet:
>
> You will eat, bye and bye,
> In that glorious land above the sky;
> Work and pray, live on hay,
> You'll get pie in the sky when you die.

PIG IN A POKE

This phrase has three related meanings:

••• A deal that is rushed into and accepted without a careful examination of details;

••• An object that hasn't been adequately appraised; *or*

••• A low-value object presented in a shifty manner intended to mask its true worth.

The expression dates back to the 1500s, when a "poke" was another word for "bag" or "sack." If a pig merchant sidled up to you with a tied poke and told you that there was a pig inside, and if you bought it without looking inside first to verify that the poke's contents were, indeed, said pig, you might be getting scamalamadingdonged. Moral of the story: under no circumstances should you purchase a pig in a poke.

The phrase is closely related to the still-used idiom "let the cat out of the bag," i.e., to blurt out or reveal a secret. Apparently, duplicitous merchants would occasionally substitute cats instead of pigs in their pokes; their unwitting customers often wouldn't discover the sham until they'd gotten home and fished the cat out of the bag.

PIGS AND WHISTLES

If you've "gone to pigs and whistles," you've fallen into utter ruin.

> Frae this they tell, as how the rent
> O' sic a room was overstent,
> The back-ga'en tenant fell a-hint,
> And coudnae stand;
>
> For he to pygs and whistles went,
> And left the land.

—Excerpt from "The Har'st Rig" (1794), Scottish poem, author unknown

PIKER

A nineteenth-century cheapskate.

PILL

This word has a variety of old incarnations that should be revisited, including:

••• A dour, tiresomely disagreeable person.

••• To go bald.

PIN YOUR EARS BACK

An instruction to listen carefully. ("Pin your ears back when you listen to the end of 'Strawberry Fields Forever,' and you'll hear all kinds of trippy things.")

PINCHPENNY

A scrooge or miser, a "piker" (see page 155).

PIPE DOWN

A quaint synonym for "hush up." One difference: "pipe down" was usually bellowed, whereas "hush" was usually issued as an exaggerated whisper.

THE PITS

"My bridesmaid dress for her wedding is the pits: poofy and fuchsia with huge bows stuck all over it." In other words, a dreary, beastly place, person, object, or state of affairs.

PIZZAZZ

A mid-century word for "dash" or "flair," used with famous gusto by iconic magazine editor Diana Vreeland. One of fashion history's most charismatic figures, Vreeland morphed from stylish housewife into the fashion editor of *Harper's Bazaar* magazine. In 1962, she commandeered *Vogue*, where she presided over the industry during that decade's "youthquake" (a term she coined) into the early 1970s.

Everything Vreeland did had dash and flair, and she was unrepentantly idiosyncratic: she rouged her cheeks *and* her earlobes, dyed her hair lacquer-black well into her advanced years, had her maid polish the tops *and* bottoms of her shoes, and toted dollar bills that were freshly ironed for her each morning. Her expressions and bon mots were equally colorful and are still quoted ("Never fear being vulgar, just boring" was one of her mantras).

It made perfect sense that she was parodied in the 1957 film *Funny Face* as bossy-yet-loveable fashion editor Maggie Prescott, and her dialogue was peppered with the word "pizzazz":

"The Quality Woman must have grace, elegance, and pizzazz."

"Give 'em the old pizzazz."

"She's got to be more than all right. She's got to have pizzazz."

SEE ALSO "CAUGHT DEAD" *and* "MARVELOUS"

THE PLAYERS

Instead of "the cast" in movie credits. Casts are for broken legs.

A COP BY ANY OTHER NAME

Old Slang for Policemen and Detectives

Lawmen have had countless less-than-flattering nicknames
over the years ("pig" springs immediately to mind),
but here are a few of the gentler ones:

Blue / blue bottle	Fuzz
Copper	Gumshoe
Cossack	John Law
Dick	Peeler
Flatfoot	Scufter
Frog	

IN THE CLINK

Historical Slang Words for "Prison"

Incarceration has likely never been a lark, but at least it *sounds* better to have spent a stint in the "pokey" instead of a plain old stinky jail. A few other old-guard penitentiary synonyms:

....

Big house

Big school

Calaboose

Can

Cooler

Family-hotel

Fancy-piece

In hoosegow

Icebox

Joint

Jug

Quod

Sheriff's hotel

Slammer

Tank

Teetotal hotel

Up the river

PLEASE THE PIGS

If all is well, or if all goes accordingly to plan: "Please the pigs, I'll get that woman to marry me before the end of the year."

A PLUGGED NICKEL

A worthless object—usually used in the early twentieth-century phrase "not worth a plugged nickel." When American coins were still made of valuable metals, people would carve out little holes in them and fill those holes—called "plugs"—with a cheaper metal. Once a coin had gone through this process, it was, of course, worthless as legal tender. An amusing observation on the topic from *The Word Detective:* "This sort of larcenous messing with currency has been popular since coins first appeared millennia ago, and Americans were plugging French, English, and other nations' coins back in the days before we had our own to plug."

fig. 21: QUICK-DRAW

PLUMPER

A very pleasing arcane word for "a lie."

POCKET-PISTOL

A liquor-filled flask.

POLITE SOCIETY

An old term for the upper class, usually shortened to just plain old "society." One dictionary definition adds the following nuance to the expression: "Polite society" is often used in a humorous capacity, and usually suggests that its members "pretend that things they consider to be unpleasant do not exist." Anyone who's ever read an Edith Wharton novel knows that polite society tends to be rather impolite behind closed doors, giving the expression an ironic tenor as well.

SEE ALSO "THE QUALITY"

POLLRUMPTIOUS

Rowdy, raucous, unruly: "A pollrumptious party."

SEE ALSO "LUMPSHIOUS" *and* "GOLLUMPUS"

POLTROON

A coward. And not just a run-of-the-mill coward, but rather a "wretched coward," a "craven," and a "dastard" (see page 52). People in the sixteenth century were great at coming up with insults, and appeared to have held cowards in particular disdain.

POODLE

A haircut. On a totally different note, the term "poodle-faker" was old British slang for "an ingratiating male."

SEE ALSO "HAIR BUTCHER"

POOR MAN'S OYSTERS

Mussels. Although anyone who's ever ordered *moules* in any of the expensive Keith McNally restaurants in New York City might question the aptness of this expression.

POTTY

Ever so slightly nuts.

SEE ALSO "KOOKY"

PRAYER BOOK

Mischievous old slang for "a deck of cards."

SEE ALSO "DEVIL'S TEETH"

fig. 22: NOTHIN' UP MY SLEEVE

PRETTY-PRETTY

A bauble or gewgaw. The term gets to the essence of such artifacts: we often want them only because they are indeed "pretty-pretty," not because they are "practical-practical."

PRETTY AS A PICTURE

No one ever said a picture of *what*, but let's assume it was a lovely sunlight- and flower-filled still life, and not something akin to Edvard Munch's *The Scream*.

A PRETTY PASS

This "pretty" phrase was anything but: riddled with sarcasm, it meant to encounter an ugly or difficult situation. "Things have come to a pretty pass: that do-it-yourself perm made all of my hair fall out."

PRICKMEDENTY

Also often written as "prickmedainty," this word signifies a finicky, affected person.

PRIME TWIG

High spirits: "After four glasses of Champagne, he was in prime twig."

PROWLER

A far more evocative, feline word for "burglar."

THE PURPLE

A term for "royalty," as illustrated by the following utterance from Queen Victoria, issued upon hearing of the demise of Prince Louis Napoléon: "To think of that dear young man, the apple of his mother's eye, born and nurtured in the purple, dying thus, is too fearful, too awful."

PURSE-PROUD

Ostentatiously proud of one's wealth. These days, one who totes an Hermès Birkin bag can be said to be purse-proud both literally and figuratively.

PUSSYFOOT

Another wonderful feline p-word: "pussyfoot" meant to tread cautiously or stealthily, or to equivocate. ("I *know* for a fact that you ate the last caramel *fleur de sel* macaroon, so stop pussyfooting around and confess!")

PUT AN OAR IN

A polite definition of this expression "to interfere." A more-to-the-point definition: "to say or do something which annoys other people because they have not asked you to join their conversation or activity" (*Cambridge Advance Learner's Dictionary and Thesaurus*).

PUT SOME HEAT UNDER IT

Speed things up: "If he's going to win this hot dog–eating contest, he'd better put some heat under it! He's still ten wieners behind."

SEE ALSO "QUICK STICKS"

PUT THAT IN YOUR PIPE AND SMOKE IT

As a verbal sparring weapon, this phrase is a cleverer alternative to "take that!" and a far classier version of our contemporary "suck on that."

PUT THE FINGER ON SOMEONE

To accuse someone of something. Also: "put the pin on someone."

PUT UP OR SHUT UP

The perfect old admonishment for those who must often deal with chronic complainers, "put up or shut up" means "either work to ameliorate a bad situation, or quit whining about it."

QUACK

Shortened from the sixteenth-century words "quacksalver" or "quacksalve," the word "quack" described a charlatan doctor or healer who went about the countryside "quacking" about his "salves" and cures. By the early 1900s, however, the definition had apparently broadened to include any old "noisy, specious cheat."

THE QUALITY

A centuries-old word for "gentry" or "aristocracy," usually used by people who do not fall into that category. "[The expression is] old-fashioned, and now vulgar," sniffed the 1891 *Dictionary of Idiomatic Phrases*. The term showed up a few times in Mark Twain's *The Adventures of Huckleberry Finn*. One example: "I set my teeth in. It was 'baker's bread'—what the quality eat—none of your low-down corn pone."

QUAVERY-WAVERY

On the fence. A more modern synonym that also showcases our continued affection for childish doublets: "wishy-washy."

SEE ALSO "NIFFY-NAFFY"

QUICK STICKS

An exclamation urging someone to hurry up ("Stop lollygagging about and get dressed, quick sticks!"). "Cutting quick sticks" meant to start out quickly. According to one source, the phrase was likely coined by seventeenth-century British sailors who beheld "the nimbleness of the Chinese in their eating without the aid of forks"; they dubbed the Chinese utensils "chopsticks" and "quick sticks."

SEE ALSO "FIRST CHOP"

QUIZ

A prying, nosy person. ("Every time that old quiz comes around, I pull the curtains and close the windows.")

QUOCKERWODGER

A marionette. Also old slang for anyone—namely a politician—whose strings are pulled by somebody else.

RACKABONES

A very skinny person. In certain upper-crust circles, a good vintage-ish synonym would be "social X-rays," a term coined for ultra-thin socialites in Tom Wolfe's 1987 satirical novel, *The Bonfire of the Vanities.*

RAGTAG AND BOBTAIL

The less desirable elements of society, about whom the 1891 *Dictionary of Idiomatic Phrases* glowers: "Those loungers about a city who are always ready to flock together and make a mob."

RAKESHAME

A libertine; a wildly disreputable, lewd person. Someone so reprehensible, in fact, that he or she is most likely to be found "raking in hell." Usually shortened to "rake" (see "Scofflaws and Scoundrels: Historical Words for Men of Ill-Repute," page 176), but the full term is so entertaining that it's worth highlighting in its own right.

RAMMISH

Odious-smelling, as in a "rammish pair of gym socks, bearing the stink of a thousand years of unwashedness."

RAN-TAN

A spree; a state of wild excitement—usually used within the phrase "on the ran-tan" or as an adverb: "He galloped ran-tan down the hill, beating his chest like a gorilla."

RANCE-SNIFFLE

It is worth including this entertaining old word just to showcase the definition given in the 1905 *Dictionary of Slang and Colloquial English*: "A mean and
dastardly piece of malignity."

RATTLECAP

A volatile person.

> Franklin at once took the measure of this rattlecap profligate . . .
> he thought it would be interesting to let [him] bubble and dribble away in
> the reckless chatter of this loathsome Lieutenant.

**—Francis Herbert Stead, *No More War!
Truth Embodied in a Tale* (1917)**

RAZZLE-DAZZLE

Variously defined as "flashy theatricality," "riotous gaiety," and a "complex
maneuver designed to confuse an opponent." In any case, hardly anyone uses
the phrase "give them the old razzle-dazzle" anymore, and it might be amusing
to resurrect it. The expression's origin is unclear, although some sources posit
the possibility that "razzle-dazzle"—and its synonym "razzmatazz"—might be
"varied reduplications of the word 'jazz.'" Razzmatazz, as one expert points
out, "once referred to old-fashioned (and by implication, 'corny') jazz and
extravagance (fuss, commotion, garishness)." But no one appears to be certain.

SEE ALSO "JAZZ" *and* "PIZZAZZ"

RIB

This word has at least three revival-worthy old-fashioned definitions:

• • • A wife. Clearly this use has biblical roots, and references Eve's emergence from Adam's rib.

• • • To tease or ridicule someone.

• • • A joke or a hoax. Invoked to indignant perfection by Jean Harlow in the 1933 film *Bombshell*: "Say, what kind of a rib is this anyway?"

RIGHT AS RAIN

Back on your feet; healthy: "Drink a hot toddy every hour on the hour, and you'll be right as rain in no time." One etymologist sensibly ventured: "The expression *must* have been invented by an Englishman."

RINKY-DINK

This early twentieth-century phrase means "shabby," "outmoded," or "insignificant" ("He picked me up for the prom in the most rinky-dink car imaginable—the muffler was dragging on the ground behind it!"). But earlier fans of the term used it as a verb that meant "to cheat." ("She gave everyone in town the rinky-dink with her sob story, and busted out of here in the middle of the night with twenty grand in tow!")

RITZ

Glitzy, da-da-dahling, ostentatious display of luxury. Best when used in the corny phrase "Put on the ritz," i.e., to give quite a show of your wealth and baubles: "Wow, she's really puttin' on the ritz tonight with that gleaming head-to-toe sequin look. It practically sears my eyes out every time I look at her."

ROLL IN THE HAY

To "firkytoodle" (see page 72) with no long-term commitment in mind.

RONYON

Courtesy of the sixteenth century, "ronyon" means a "mangy creature." It would make an excellent, inscrutable way to refer to your neighbor's smelly, endlessly yapping dog.

ROT

I.e., "bunk" (see page 28); a very Hemingway-ish word. It appears with drunken regularity—no fewer than a million times, in fact —in his iconic 1926 novel *The Sun Also Rises*, usually courtesy of jezebel Brett Ashley:

> "What rot, I could hear Brett say it. What rot!
> When you were with the English, you got into the habit
> of using English expressions in your thinking."

ROTTEN TO THE CORE

I.e., a "bad apple" (see page 17).

ROUND HEELS

A "round-heeled" creature purportedly had a casual relationship with her virtue (i.e., it's easy to roll her onto her back). The 1823 tome *Grose's Classical Dictionary of the Vulgar Tongue* provides an even crasser synonym: "Short-heeled wench," i.e., "a girl apt to fall on her back."

fig. 23: MAYBE JUST A QUICK ONE
WHILE HE'S AWAY

ROWDYDOWDY

Not to be confused with Howdy Doody, a marionette cowboy who spoke in falsetto tones in front of a vast national television audience between 1947 and 1960. Rather, "rowdydowdy" meant "boisterous" or "uproarious," and was considered an indecent term. All the more reason to bring it back.

RUFFLES

Handcuffs.

RUMBUSTIOUS

"Rowdydowdiness" (see above) of a rambunctious variety. The word "Rum*bump*tious," on the other hand, meant "haughty" or "pompous." Perhaps the two words could be combined—"rumbumpbustious" to describe a pretentious, obnoxious person hell-bent on having an uproarious time.

RUMP AND STUMP

Through and through: "If he were to sell it rump and stump, once for all, he would be selling himself, converting himself from a free man into a slave, from an owner of a commodity into a commodity" (Karl Marx, *Das Capital,* 1906).

SEE ALSO "DYED-IN-THE-WOOL"

RUSTY-FUSTY-DUSTY

A more rollicking way of describing someone who's dirty and stinky.

SADDLE ONE'S NOSE

To don spectacles.

SEE ALSO "BARNACLES" *and* "BLINKERS"

SAND IN ONE'S CRAW

Courage. Used memorably in *The Adventures of Huckleberry Finn* by Mark Twain (who also gets snaps for transforming the past tense of "climb" into "clumb" in this passage):

> I got to camp I warn't feeling very brash, there warn't much sand in my craw; but I says, this ain't no time to be fooling around. So I got all my traps into my canoe again so as to have them out of sight, and I put out the fire and scattered the ashes around to look like an old last year's camp, and then clumb a tree.

SAP

A fool or a dupe (or, in equally quaint vernacular, a "dope"). Divine as an adjective: "sappy"—which is usually used to describe something that is "foolishly sentimental." ("Everyone keeps on gushing about how amazing that old Ali MacGraw movie *Love Story* is, but I think it's totally sappy.")

SAUCE

Booze. One never "sips" sauce delicately, pinky finger crooked; rather, one "hits" it:

> "You really think it's cool for you to hit the sauce with a bun in the oven?"

—Steve Zissou in the film *The Life Aquatic with Steve Zissou* (2004)

SAUCE-BOX

A forward, bold person; i.e., a "whippersnapper" (see page 212).

SAWBONES

Old slang for "doctor." Really gets down to the essence of the vocation.

fig. 24: SAY WHEN

SCANDAL BROTH

Tea. The reference is to the scandal-mongering "gossip held by some of the womenkind over their cups which cheer but [do] not inebriate," according to the 1895 *Dictionary of Phrase and Fable: Giving the Derivation, Source, or Origin of Common Phrases, Allusions, and Words That Have a Tale to Tell*. Equally pleasing related old synonyms include "chatter broth" and "prattle broth."

SCANTIES

Particularly apt today, since "scanties" (i.e., underpants) are so scant among example-setting young starlets.

SCAPEGRACE

A nineteenth-century term for a tirelessly unscrupulous person. Some sources think it meant someone who "escapes" the "grace" of God, thanks to his rascally-ness.

SCARCE AS HEN'S TEETH

Extremely rare or impossible to find. As anyone who's ever fished around in a hen's mouth can tell you, these birds don't have teeth—hence the sensible-ness of this American expression. It likely harkens back to colonial times.

SCATTERLING

A vagabond. Also once known as a "shackaback."

SCHOOL OF HARD KNOCKS

Usually this early twentieth-century phrase referred to the rather unpleasant-yet-valuable lessons dealt out by life's unhappy experiences. Yet sometimes it was invoked in a macro-sense to mean "life" in general. In any case, the term "hard knocks" was later re-popularized by the song "It's the Hard-Knock Life," sung by a passel of bedraggled orphans in the 1977 Broadway musical *Annie*, and again in 1998 when rapper Jay-Z released his album "Hard Knock Life," featuring the song "Hard Knock Life (Ghetto Anthem)"—which included a chorus sampled from the original *Annie* soundtrack.

SCOFFLAW

An irascible person who habitually defies or "scoffs at" the law. According to etymologist Douglas Harper, "scofflaw" was "the winning entry in a national contest during Prohibition to coin a word to characterize a person who drinks illegally, chosen from more than 25,000 entries." The stakes had been high: the winning prize was $200—quite a chunk of change in those days.

SCRAPE ACQUAINTANCE

To insinuate oneself into an acquaintance. The term smacks of opportunistic friend-making, probably by an unwelcome, overly-familiar person. There is no shortage of creatures who devote themselves to this practice today; let's revive this apt expression right away.

SECOND BANANA

Most people still know the old term "second fiddle," or a person who has to serve in an adjunct capacity; the expression refers to the non-leading violin (or fiddle) in a quartet or the second violin section of an orchestra. An even better vintage phrase: "second banana," who is secondary to a "top banana" (such as the chicly scandalous Holly Golightly, heroine of Truman Capote's 1947 book *Breakfast at Tiffany's*, who proudly proclaims, "I'm always top banana in the shock department").

SCOFFLAWS AND SCOUNDRELS

Historical Words for Men of Ill-Repute

The sheer volume of old terms for "knavish" men implies that they
abounded in bygone eras—as they do today.

Blackleg	Fustilarian	Rascal
Bounder	Gulf-spin	Rip
Cad	Gutter-blood	Rogue
Cullion	Heel	Ruffian
Cutter	Lout	Scallywag
	Lurcher	Scamp
	Rake	Scapegrace
	Ramper	Scullion
	Rapscallion	Varlet

SEE YOU LATER, ALLIGATOR

A parting phrase from the 1950s, invariably responded to with:
"In a while, crocodile." Both expressions were popularized by
the 1955 Bill Haley & His Comets song "See You Later, Alligator,"
which was a big hit on the swing dancing circuit.

SEE ALSO "FAREWELL"

fig. 25: UNTIL NEXT TIME

SEEDY

Meaning disreputable, run-down, or degraded; often used in conjunction
with the word "hotel."

SEEK-SORROW

Everyone knows the type: a "seek-sorrow" is a person who's always searching
out drama, or a reason to be woebegone.

SEE ALSO "BORROW TROUBLE"

SET YOUR CAP AT SOMEONE

In the eighteenth century, when a woman was hell-bent on "catching" a
particular man, she was "setting her cap" at him. The phrase was discussed
in the 1811 Jane Austen novel, *Sense and Sensibility:*

> "That is an expression, Sir John," said Marianne, warmly,
> "which I particularly dislike. I abhor every common-place phrase by which
> wit is intended; and 'setting one's cap at a man,' or 'making a conquest,'
> are the most odious of all. Their tendency is gross and illiberal."

SHAKE A LEG

As in, "get a move on."

SEE ALSO "QUICK STICKS" *and* "PUT SOME HEAT UNDER IT"

SILVER SCREEN SYNONYMS

Historical Words and Phrases for "Movie"

All of these terms make filmgoing sound so compelling and animated,
while today's word "movie" largely conjures up images of stale popcorn
in mall theaters. Let's revive some of these synonyms and reclaim
some of the glamour of the old-fashioned theatergoing experience.

Flick

Motion picture

Moving picture

Photoplay

Picture show

Shadow play

Talkie

Talking picture

SHAPE UP OR SHIP OUT

Get yourself up to par, or beat it out of town.

SEE ALSO "PUT UP OR SHUT UP"

SHEEP'S EYES

"Making sheep's eyes" at someone means to gaze at him or her amorously.

SHILLAGALEE

A loafer or "ne'er-do-well" (see page 138).

SHILLY-SHALLY

To fritter time away, stall, or vacillate in an annoying manner.

SHOOT THE BREEZE

A synonym for "beat one's gums" (see page 18).

SHOWBOAT

Meaning a person who is behaving in an outrageous or flamboyant manner. This wonderful old-fashioned word somehow manages to make its subject sound particularly ridiculous, and therein lies its allure.

SEE ALSO "DREAMBOAT"

"WHORESON CULLIONLY BARBER-MONGER"

Insults Scripted by the Great Bard William Shakespeare

Next time you need to insult someone, but need to do so in a highbrow manner, consider resurrecting one of the following Shakespearean taunts—you shan't find anything more deliciously nasty in any modern parlance.

"A foul and pestilent congregation of vapours" – *Hamlet*

"A slippery and subtle knave" – *Othello*

"Base ignoble wretch" – *King Henry VI*

"Bastardly rogue" – *King Henry IV*

"Bolting-hutch of beastliness" – *King Henry IV*

"Brazen-faced varlet" – *King Lear*

"Contemptuous base-born callet" – *King Henry VI*

"Crooked-pated old cuckoldy ram" – *As You Like It*

"Dull and muddy-mottled rascal" – *Hamlet*

"False murd'rous coward" – *King Henry VI*

"Fat-kidneyed rascal" – *King Henry IV*

"Filthy worsted-stocking knave" – *King Lear*

"Foul indigested lump" – *Henry IV* (Also available: "foul slut," "foul wretch," and "foul wrinkled witch")

"Freckled whelp hag-born" – *The Tempest*

"Hag of all despite" – *King Henry VI*

"Knotty-pated fool" – *Henry IV*

"Loathesome leper" – *Henry VI*

"Mad mustachio purple-hued maltworm" – *Henry IV*

"Most toad-spotted traitor" – *King Lear*

"Peevish brat" – *King Richard III*

"Pigeon-livered" – *Hamlet*

"Poor, base, rascally, cheating, lack-linen mate" – *Henry IV*

"Prating coxcomb" – *King Henry V*

"You whoreson loggerhead" – *Love's Labour Lost*

· ·

And if you are feeling particularly vehement, you can hurl
the following exclamation at the subject of your ire, which comes
to us courtesy of Kent's tirade toward Oswald in *King Lear*:

· ·

"[You are a] knave; a rascal; an eater of broken meats; a
base, proud, shallow, beggarly, three-suited, hundred-pound,
filthy, worsted-stocking knave; a lily-livered, action-taking
knave, a whoreson, glass-gazing, super-serviceable finical
rogue; one-trunk-inheriting slave; one that wouldst be a
bawd, in way of good service, and art nothing but the com-
position of a knave, beggar, coward, pandar, and the son and
heir of a mongrel bitch: one whom I will beat into clamorous
whining, if thou deniest the least syllable of thy addition."

SHRINKING VIOLET

A painfully shy person. *The American Heritage Dictionary of Idioms* states that "the precise allusion is unclear, since violets thrive under a variety of conditions and often are considered a garden weed." However, some kinds of violets have proved less hardy, such as the Parma violet. An exotic branch of the violet family that gives off a beautiful, strong fragrance, Parmas were often worn by Victorian ladies in a bouquet tied to the waist or pinned to the bosom. These sweet, fickle, hard-to-cultivate flowers sadly went out of fashion as both plantings and accessories after World War I.

SKINFLINT

A mean, low-down miser, i.e., the type of person "who would skin a flint to save or gain something." A related expression: "skin a flea for its hide."

SEE ALSO "PINCHPENNY"

SKITTERWIT

A flighty person; also often written as "skitterbrain." The word seems to denote someone with a rather abbreviated attention span; what could be more applicable in today's technology-sponsored ADD society? Perhaps we could even update it to "*Twitter*brain."

SLAPHAPPY

Giddy, dazed, or generally bemused. A 1920s term that "comes from the sport of boxing, which has produced too many men who act like this because they've taken too many blows to the head," according to the *Encyclopedia of Word and Phrase Origins*.

SLATTERN

Another one of those divine words that sound like what they mean: "a slovenly, untidy woman or girl," or "a slut; harlot." Since the word came up, "harlot" is quite wonderful too; it sounds so dismissive and indignant. As in, "Oh, don't pay a *scrap* of attention to that harlot."

SLAY

As in, "Oh, Myrtle, you simply *slay* me! You're such a card."

SLIBBER-SLABBER

Careless: "You could not have been more slibber-slabber when making my fake ID. Look, you turned me into a seventy-four-year-old man, and I'm only seventeen!" Note: this phrase is most certainly *not* to be confused with "slip-slop," which means "a mistake."

SLUBBERDEGULLION

A 1913 definition of this term is almost as amusing as the term itself: "a paltry, dirty, sorry wretch."

SLUMGULLION

The sound tells you exactly what it meant, although there are a dozen different definitions. For Twain a slumgullion was a weak tea with "too much dish-rag, sand and old bacon-rind." For Melville, it was the waste from whale processing; for miners the detritus from mining ore; for diners, a sorry excuse for stew. Whatever it was, a slumgullion was always as unpleasant as it sounds, and it certainly beats any modern version of the word that I can think of.

RUTH REICHL • LONGTIME EDITOR, *GOURMET* MAGAZINE; AUTHOR OF *TENDER AT THE BONE* AND *GARLIC AND SAPPHIRES*

SLUMGUZZLE

To pull the wool over someone's eyes.

SLY BOOTS

A "smart aleck" (see below): "If you're such a sly boots, let's see you come up with a way out of this mess." Also great: "surly-boots," i.e., a "grumpy, morose fellow."

SEE ALSO "CLEVER CLOGS"

SMALL POTATOES

A subversively belittling synonym for "a nobody" or something that's no big deal. ("Oh, you needn't worry about him upstaging you; he's so small potatoes that the farmer wouldn't even bother digging him up during a famine.")

SMART ALECK

An annoying know-it-all. And while we're at it, let's also bring back "smart nose," "smarty pants," "smarty boots," "wise-guy," "wiseacre," and "swellhead."

SMELL A RAT

To get the sense that something is wrong, usually that someone has been dishonest in some way. Also fun: "Smell something fishy."

SNAKE IN THE GRASS

A comeback-worthy expression because of its specificity: "A treacherous person, especially one who feigns friendship" (*Random House Dictionary*). The closest contemporary synonym we have is "frenemy."

SNAZZY

The words usually used to define "snazzy" are equally dorky-yet-endearing: "flashy" or "fancy." One etymologist theorizes that the word was originally a "blend of snappy and jazzy."

SNIRP

Where *has* this deliciously nasty word been hiding for the last few centuries? "Snirp"—which manages to combine the best of "nerd" and "twerp" and adds in a drop of insulting sibilance—means "an undersized, contemptible wretch," according to *A Dictionary of Slang and Colloquial English* (1905).

SNUB-DEVIL

A parson or preacher.

SOBER-WATER

Seltzer.

fig. 26: TO YOUR HEALTH

SOLEMNCHOLY

Everyone still knows the word "melancholy" ("a gloomy state of mind"), but fewer may be familiar with the old world "solemncholy" ("seriousness, gravity")—which somehow seems far more expressive than its modern counterpart, "solemnity."

SORE

Huffy.

A SORRY SIGHT

"She made *quite* the entrance, shimmering in all of that frippery. But three bourbons later, that girl was the sorriest sight you'd ever seen."

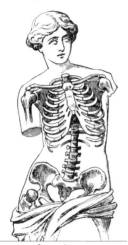

fig. 27: I'M THINKING OF
HAVING SOME WORK DONE

SOUL BUTTER

Flattery.

SOUL-CASE

The body.

SOURDOUGH

Counterfeit money; a clever riff on the slang word
"dough."

SEE ALSO "COLD HARD CASH: TERMS FOR 'MONEY'
OVER THE CENTURIES" (PAGE 131)

SOURPUSS

A scowling, grouchy person. His other contemporaneous names included
"gloomy Gus" or "picklepuss."

SPARK

Sometimes this denoted a "foppish young man," (see "fop" on page 74),
but as a verb, it also meant "to woo" as used in the 1939 film *Gone with
the Wind*:

KATHLEEN
What's your sister so mad about, Scarlett: you sparkin' her beau?

SCARLETT
As if I couldn't get a better beau than that old maid in britches.

SPECTACLES

The word "glasses" has very nerdy overtones:

> *Men seldom make passes*
> *At girls who wear glasses.*

—Dorothy Parker

Yet the word "spectacles" sounds sweet and charming.

SPINDLE-SHANKS

A set of skinny legs.

SEE ALSO "RACKABONES"

SPLENDIFEROUS

A rollicking sixteenth-century upgrade of the word "splendid."

SPOONEY

To be cuckoo about someone:

> I went spooney on her. I am spoons still. I told her that until I met her again, I would send her a bunch of violets every day.

— I.T. Hecker, "His Irish Cousins" (1878)

SQUARE

A conservative, prim, old-fashioned, uncool bore.

SQUEAL

A particularly insulting synonym for "tattle."

STAB-RAG

A tailor.

SEE ALSO "HAIR-BUTCHER" *and* "IVORIES"

STAMPERS

Shoes or legs. Amusing, related term: a "stamp-crab" was a "lumpish walker."

SEE ALSO "BEETLE-CRUSHER"

STEP OUT

To cheat on one's spouse: "Eunice caught Elmer stepping out and gave him a batty-fanging of a lifetime. I swear, that man will never walk right again."

STICK IN THE MUD

This can either mean an "old fogy" or a "narrow-minded person" (i.e., some-one with his feet mired in mud and unable/unwilling to move). Perhaps the best definition of the phrase comes courtesy of *The Dictionary of Idiomatic Phrases* (1891): "A person who is wholly without the spirit of enterprise or adventure." The term dates back to the 1500s, along with "stuck in the briars," which proved to have less staying power.

STRAIN AT A GNAT

To make a big fuss or "kerfuffle" (see page 109) about something wholly insignificant: "Ye blind guides, which strain at a gnat and swallow a camel" (Matthew 23:24).

STRETCHER

A hot one (see page 97).

SEE ALSO "WHOPPER" *and* "FIB"

STRUMPET

If it's good enough for Shakespeare, it's good enough for us. Much ado has been made over the derogatory names women call each other, largely because we've yet to reclaim any of them as our own. Not really. No matter the proud delivery, stating "I'm/she's such a slut" always rings cruel and exaggerated. "Strumpet" has a sense of whimsy about it. It has an affectionately sophisticated ring and it's old-fashioned nature gives it tempered impact. Plus it sounds an awful lot like "crumpet," a word that has also gone out of regular circulation . . . but whose basic ingredients can still be spotted through store windows, sold and purchased for consumption.

SLOANE CROSLEY • AUTHOR, *HOW DID YOU GET THIS NUMBER* AND *I WAS TOLD THERE'D BE CAKE*

STRUT-NODDY

"A mincing fool." This definition from the early 1900s certainly doesn't mince any words.

STUFFED SHIRT

This term has various definitions, but the synonym that appears in most definitions is "pompous" ("an overly formal or pompous person," "a pompous, self-satisfied, and inflexible person," and so on).

SEE ALSO "FUDDY DUDDY"

STUMP-OF-THE-GUTTER

An eighteenth-century term of contempt that could mean anything from "dumpy" to "squat."

SUP WITH PLUTO

To "join the majority" (see page 107), or die. Pluto was the Roman god of the underworld and oversaw the realm of the dead. When "supping" with him at Chez Afterlife, there likely would have been two things on the menu: maggots and vultures.

SWASHBUCKLER

This archaic word means "a swaggering bully or ruffian." You're not supposed to like bullies or ruffians, but something about the word "swashbuckler" makes you want to invite one to a party. The word is also sometimes defined as a "flamboyant adventurer" and a "daredevil"—both of which are equally guest-list-worthy categories.

SWEAR WORD

Delightfully prim: "Percival, you have the mouth of a sailor. I simply will not tolerate such swear words under my roof—on a *Sunday*, no less."

SWELL

This old word is especially good in sarcastic use: "The toilet overflowed? Oh, that's just *swell*."

TALK THROUGH ONE'S HAT

To speak authoritatively on a subject about which one knows nothing. The expression's origin is unclear, although *The Phrase Finder* uncovered an early instance of the term (courtesy of *Slang and Its Analogues*, 1888): "Dis is only a bluff dey're makin'—see! Dey're talkin' tru dere hats!" *The Phrase Finder* surmises the utterance could *only* be American, and likely originated on these shores.

TARADIDDLE

A falsehood—but just a wee little one. More of a fib than a lie.

SEE ALSO "STRETCHER"

TARNATION

A rootin' tootin' version of the exclamation "damnation!" Says one etymologist of the eighteenth-century Americanism: The word was "influenced by [the word] 'tarnal' (1790), from the phrase by the 'Eternal' (God)." As everyone knows, "damnation" has long since been truncated to "damn," but rarely has someone spit out the word "tarn!" when having a hissy fit or tantrum. But there's still time to start a new trend.

TATTLETALE

A squealer (see page 188).

TEA VOIDER

A simultaneously crass and prim old expression for "chamber pot."

TEETH OUTWARDS

If something was described as being "from the teeth outwards," it was "without significance" or "merely superficial." ("Everybody is compelled by politeness to 'talk from his teeth outwards,' instead of from his heart or mind"—*The Spectator*, 1890.)

THAT'S THE WAY THE COOKIE CRUMBLES

This seems like an especially cruel old saying—after all, what could be more consoling and comforting than a cookie? And then it is used in this callous manner, to describe the unfairness of life.

SEE ALSO "SCHOOL OF HARD KNOCKS"

THICK AS THIEVES

Closely allied; in cahoots. Probably related to the similar, still-popular expression "partners in crime."

THUNDERATION

A splendid alternative to "tarnation" (see page 193). Other great old "thunder"-related exclamations:

BY THUNDER!

THUNDER-AND-LIGHTNING!

THUNDER-AND-TURF!

Sometimes even a plain old "Thunder!" sufficed.

TICKLE-BRAIN

A very strong drink.

TICKLED PINK

In other words: thrilled to tatters and pleased as punch. Also good: "tickled to death." Both powdery phrases were likely most frequently invoked by mid-century mothers-in-law during games of bridge.

TIE ONE ON

To have a drink—or ten. In other words, to get good and plastered. Another one of those "origin unclear" words. Some sources wonder if it dates to the old American West, where a "cowboy would have to tie up his horse to a hitching post before he could go into the saloon and get drunk." This likely isn't the origin, but it's still a pleasing visual.

TIED TO APRON STRINGS

When a man was "under the thumb" of his wife or mother, he was said to be tied to her apron strings. This phrase was in use for hundreds of years, and was still popular in the first half of the twentieth century. Consider the lyrics of the song "St. Louis Blues" (1914), popularized by jazz legend Billie Holiday:

> *St. Louis woman with her diamond rings*
> *Pulls that man around by her apron strings*
> *If it wasn't for powder and her store-bought hair*
> *That man I love wouldn't have gone nowhere*

TIGHT-LACED

Exceedingly proper—even puritanical. This word—and its sister, "strait-laced"—evoke a tightly laced corset, which would, of course, create quite a bit of rigidity in its wearer.

TIGHTWAD

A humorously derisive synonym for "cheapskate," someone who keeps a tight fist around his wad of cash.

TIP-TOPPER

The old phrase "tip-top" meant "first rate" or "the best" ("Thelma, that baked Alaska is tip-top, I tell you"), but a "tip-topper" meant "a well-dressed man." It's amazing how many words there were for this curious, now-rare breed of men in bygone eras.

SEE ALSO "BIT-OF-STUFF," "DANDIPRAT," *and* "SPARK"

TIP OVER THE PERCH

To kick the bucket (see page 110).

TIPPYBOBS

The upper classes. These days popularly referred to as "the one percent."

SEE ALSO "THE PURPLE" *and* "THE QUALITY"

TISTY-TOSTY

Swaggering or boastful: "You should have *seen* how tisty-tosty he was about his new gold tooth! And it wasn't even right in the front; no one will ever even notice it."

TO-DO

This term appears to have had two slightly different meanings: firstly, it could signify a big ol' ruckus, disturbance, or difficult situation. Otherwise, it meant a "fuss." ("Those poor things: They made such a to-do over that mermaid parade float and it *still* looked ghastly.")

TOGGERY

If someone told you in the nineteenth century that you had smashing or admirable "toggery," he was complimenting you on your wardrobe. What a spirited alternative to the plain, dowdy word "clothes"—utterly comeback-worthy. Also wonderful is the expression "togged out to the nines," meaning "beautifully dressed."

TOM, DICK, OR HARRY

This phrase was usually incomplete unless it appeared as "*every* Tom, Dick, or Harry" or "*any* Tom, Dick, or Harry." The poor gentlemen being described in this expression are stand-ins for "nobodies," or anonymous, interchangeable people ("He *claims* that he's my husband, but I don't know him from any other Tom, Dick, or Harry!"). The term likely has its origin in the sixteenth century, and various common male names have been subbed in over the years, such as "Jack." The bottom line: no matter how pleasant Tom, Dick, and Harry might be when you get to know them, you don't want to be compared to them.

fig. 28: IS THIS THING ON?

TOM LONG

A boringly longwinded storyteller; an utter windbag. The phrase has also meant "a wearisome long time." In either case, weariness abounds when it comes to ol' Tom Long.

TOMFOOL

How "ridiculously silly or foolish" people were described in the fourteenth century. The "Tom" part of the word probably comes from the generic use of the name, as a stand-in for an anonymous person (see "Tom, Dick, or Harry"). "Tomfoolery" (silly behavior) is a great pleasure to say, and it still abounds in the modern world, making this term equally revival-worthy.

TOMORROW-COME-NEVER

A day that will never arrive, akin to "a cold day in Hell."

TOOTH MUSIC

The sound of loud chewing. This is unlikely to sound like Mozart to the person sitting next to you, but to each his own.

TOP DRAWER

First chop (see page 72).

TOP OF THE MORNING

A chipper, breakfast-time exclamation—and a grand alternative to "good morning."

TOPLINER

A 1920s word describing someone "so important as to be named at or near the top of a newspaper item, advertisement, or the like." Often used as theater slang for the headlining performer of the evening, as shown in an amusing 1936 Noël Coward skit called "Red Peppers: An Interlude with Music." Below, a husband-and-wife vaudeville team quarrel with each other backstage about their fellow performers:

GEORGE:
What's the matter with Mabel Grace?

LILY:
Ask the public, dear, just ask the public.

GEORGE:
Mabel Grace . . . may be a bit long in the tooth now,
but she's a bigger star than you'll ever be, so there!

LILY:
You make me sick, sucking up to the topliners.

TOPSY-TURVY

In utter disarray; upside-down. A very old term often traced back to the early 1500s, but was "probably in popular use from an earlier period," according to one source. There has never been a time since the 1500s when the world *hasn't* felt topsy-turvy, so there was never any reason for the term to fall out of fashion.

TOT

A small child, i.e., a totterer who tottles about. Also cute: the old synonym "tyke"—although long ago the word apparently had less-than-pleasant connotations ("a cur, mongrel" or "a low, contemptible person").

SEE ALSO "ANKLE-BITER" *and* "CHATTERBOX"

TOTTY-HEADED

Harebrained (see page 92).

TOUGH BEANS

As in, "That's just too bad."

> Do I detect a look of disapproval in your eye? Well, tough beans, buddy, 'cause that's the way it's going to be.

—Holly Golightly in the 1961 film *Breakfast at Tiffany's*

fig. 29: MORE IS MORE

TRAMPOOSE

To clomp around heavily.

TRUE AS STEEL

Faithful and steadfast.

TUG-MUTTON

A delightfully gross old term for "glutton."

TUNNY

This word was used in cookbooks well into the 1960s. It's unclear how "tunny" came to be known exclusively as "tuna," a rather lumpy word in comparison. It seems much sweeter to give a child a sandwich filled with "tunny" than "tuna."

TURKEY

A benevolent synonym for "fool" or a "naïve, inept person."

TURN OVER A NEW LEAF

To start anew. This expression refers to turning a page—or "leaf"—in a book, revealing a fresh, clean page on the other side. British newspaper *The Independent* recently featured the phrase in a mischievous article about old jokes:

> Oscar Wilde comes out of prison and checks into a hotel, where he is seen going to his room with one of the hotel's page boys. He is stopped by the hotel manager, who says: "Oh, Mr. Wilde— I thought you were going to turn over a new leaf!" "So I am," says Wilde, "but I think I'll just get to the bottom of this page first . . ."

TURN-BACK

A coward. Also: "turn-tail."

TWENTY-THREE SKIDOO

To "23-skidoo" meant to "beat it," "scram," or "get while the getting is good." There seem to be no fewer than ten thousand unconfirmed theories about the phrase's origins—but regardless of its birthplace, it zipped into the national vernacular during the 1920s and into countless literary works after that, including the books *Cheaper by the Dozen* (1948) and *A Tree Grows in Brooklyn* (1943), and William S. Burroughs's 1967 short story "23-Skidoo."

TWERP

Yet another fun-to-say vintage word for a "fool" of the insignificant variety.

SEE ALSO "SNIRP"

TWIT

A twerp.

TWITCHETTY

Nervous and fidgety.

TWITTER

This may seem like an odd inclusion, considering the ubiquity of the modern social media powerhouse Twitter. Yet in the old days, someone who was "all atwitter" was in a "state of tremulous excitement." It's one of those words that truly sounds like what it means, and it would be nice to have this quainter connotation floating about again.

SEE ALSO "SKITTERWIT"

TWO-BIT

Cheap, inferior, and/or small-time. Long ago, "two-bits" were equal to twenty-five cents. The term was recently revived in the 2001 Wes Anderson film *The Royal Tenenbaums*, when main character Royal Tenenbaum discovers that his estranged wife is considering marrying a suitor:

ROYAL:
I mean, Lord knows I've had my share of infidelities,
but she's still my wife. And no damn two-bit, chartered accountant
is going to change that.

TZING-TZING

An obsolete but zippy exclamation meaning "excellent" or "great."

UNDERDRAWERS

It's simply funnier than "underwear," which is reason enough to bring it back.

UNMENTIONABLES

Same as "underdrawers." Equally entertaining synonyms include "unutterables," "unhintables," and "unwhisperables."

UP A CREEK WITH NO PADDLE

In a pickle (see page 102).

UP A TREE

The British version: "up a gum tree." A curious expression that means two opposite things: on one hand, it indicates someone who's in a rather difficult situation, and on the other, it is sometimes invoked to describe a person at ease. It's really a glass-half-empty vs. glass-half-full scenario: a squirrel chased up a tree by a hungry wolf could either be seen as trapped, or safely out of reach. Depends on that squirrel's attitude, one supposes.

UPPER STORY

The head. The expression "unfurnished in the upper story" usually meant "cuckoo" (see page 48).

SEE ALSO "ATTIC SALT"

UPPISH

Arrogant and snooty: "She certainly has been uppish since her picture ran in *Vogue*—even though it only showed the back of her head!"

UPSET THE APPLECART

To cause trouble or difficulties, or upset the norm. The image of hundreds of apples tumbling across a floor perfectly illustrates the chaos that often results from challenging the status quo.

UPSODOWN

Topsy-turvy (see page 199). Another old version: "upsy-turvy."

VARLET

One of these terms that took a downward turn somewhere along the way. In the late 1400s, a "varlet" was a page to a knight—which sounds like a fairly honorable, chivalrous occupation. However, by the 1500s, it denoted a "knavish rascal"; a "rapscallion."

VARMINT

In the eighteenth century, this meant a "naughty boy" or an "objectionable, troublesome person." Layer in the obvious modern rodent connotations, and you have a uniquely descriptive insult.

VEALY

Immature; "calf-ish."

VENTILATOR

A play or cast of actors so bad that it empties out the house. This term likely would have been enjoyed by Dorothy Parker, the most wittily vicious drama critic in modern history; as her biographer Marion Meade wrote, "theatrical producers viewed her as a piranha and dreaded the sight of her tiptoeing down the aisles." Another likely appreciator would have been Parker's fictional counterpart Waldo Lydecker—played by Clifton Webb in the 1944 film *Laura*—in which he boasts: "I don't use a pen. I write with a goose quill dipped in venom."

VENTURER

A harlot.

VIRAGO

One of the few words for which the contemporary definition ("a loud-voiced, ill-tempered, scolding woman") is as emphatic and illustrative as old-guard ones ("a masculine, violent woman, or a great two-handed female").

VIXENLY

On the subject of women with unpleasant dispositions, a "vixenly" (or "vixenish") creature could be relied upon to be "snarling," "quarrelsome," and "snappish."

VOWEL-MAULER

An annoying mumbler.

WAGTAIL

"A lewd woman," according to *Grose's Classical Dictionary of the Vulgar Tongue* (1823). The word conjures up such a humorously specific image that it seems worth including.

WASPISH

Irascible—like an ornery wasp. Not to be confused with "waspiness" of the White Anglo-Saxon Protestant variety—although WASPs do reserve their right to be "waspish" in the old sense of the word as well.

WASTREL

A wonderfully descriptive yet underused synonym for "ne'er-do-well" (see page 136).

WATER WORKS

A lady's tears—usually ones that are being beheld by an unsympathetic audience:

> Hazel broke down completely then and sobbed, with her pretty face buried in Delia's golden cushions. Delia stood by frowning for a moment. "You'll ruin those cushions," she said. "Do turn off the water works and tell me what has happened, and where is Barry."

—Ruth Mildred Ayres, *The Marriage of Barry Wicklow* (1921)

A woman prone to turning on the water works was said to be "watery-headed" in the old days.

WAX

A tantrum or rage: "Let's hide his nose-hair clipper and really get him in a wax."

WEAR THE WILLOW

To be abandoned by one's lover or mistress.

> Shee that long true love profest,
> She hath robb'd my heart of rest;
> For she a new love loves, not mee;
> Which makes me weare the willowe-tree.

> Thy hard happ doth mine appease,
> Companye doth sorrowe ease;Yet, Phillis, still I pine for thee,
> And still must weare the willowe-tree.

**—Excerpt from "The Willow Tree: A Pastoral Dialogue,"
English poem, author unknown**

WEE-JEE

Something that's top-notch: "Simon, that cravat is a wee-jee. Can't recall when I've seen a finer one."

WELL-THATCHED

Term describing an admirably thick head of hair— something that men have been grateful for throughout time. Contemporary men proud of their "well-thatched" coifs would likely appreciate such an old-timey compliment.

WELL, I NEVER

Amusingly Quaint Reaction Phrases

Any of these rather grandmotherly exclamations would make splendid
conversational alternatives to today's commonly uttered responses
("Shut up!" . . . "No way!") upon hearing surprising information.

By golly	I never did
Dearie me	Land's sake
Do tell	My, my
Geewhilikins	No fooling
Good night, nurse	Pray tell
Gracious me	Words fail me
Heavens to Betsy	You don't say
I do declare	

fig. 30: A PLEASURE DOING BUSINESS

WET BARGAIN

A deal made when all parties involved are drinking, and therefore one that is likely to be null and void the next morning (if it is remembered at all).

WET BEHIND THE EARS

Naïve. Someone who's "wet behind the ears" has as much savvy as a baby so recently born that it's still wet. The term is admittedly a bit gross, but gets the point across vividly.

WHEN PIGS FLY

An animal-world synonym for "tomorrow-come-never" (see page 198).

WHIPPERSNAPPER

A perfectly wonderful word from the late 1600s, meaning "an unimportant but offensively presumptuous person, especially a young one." We certainly still have plenty of such creatures around today; why not revive this amusingly insulting term for them?

WHIPSTER

A clever, sharp-witted lad.

WHISTLE DOWN THE WIND

Talking for the sake of talking, and saying nothing of note while doing so.

WHISTLING DIXIE

To talk about something more rosily than circumstances merit, or indulge in unrealistic fantasies. As per the *Random House Dictionary*, the expression was probably based on the idea of Southerners marching during the Civil War and whistling the folk song "Dixie" as they fought their losing battle:

> *I wish I was in the land of cotton,*
> *Old times they are not forgotten;*
> *Look away! Look away! Look away! Dixie land.*

WHITE SATIN

A prettified term for "gin," largely used by ladies in bygone eras. Gin also went by "light-blue," "blue-ruin," "duke," "royal poverty," "right-sort," "ladies' finger," "mother's milk," "cat's water," and "clap-of-thunder," among many other aliases.

WHOPPER

A "taradiddle" on steroids (see page 193). An equally great "W" synonym: "whizzer."

WIFFLE-WOFFLES

Having them meant being "down in the dumps." But the term seems curative, somehow: after all, just saying "I have the wiffle-woffles today" is bound to cheer you up. *Breakfast at Tiffany's* heroine Holly Golightly might have fared far better if she'd used this expression instead of the alarming phrase "the mean reds."

WIGANOWNS

An entertaining eighteenth-century word for a man who sports large wigs.

WILL O' THE WISP

Anything that deludes or deceives—or a person who is impossible to catch.
The term was first used in the seventeenth century, and was often described
as a ghostly light seen by travelers at night, especially over bogs, swamps,
or marshes. This light, which resembled a flickering lamp, receded when
approached and lured travelers away from the safe paths.

WILLY-NILLY

Awfully disorganized or sloppy: "They claim that dance performance was
high art,   but to me it looked like a lot of people running willy-nilly around
on the stage in their underwear." Apparently this term was derived from
the early seventeenth-century expression "will ye, nill ye"—or "whether you
will or not." One etymologist notes that there was a similar phrase in Latin:
nolens volens.

WIN AT A CANTER

To achieve victory easily, without having to break one's stride.

WINDOWS

Peepers (see page 151).

WISE UP

As in, "get smart." Those being urged to "wise up" were usually slow to
"get the drift" (see page 81) in the first place.

WISECRACK

It's amusing to see contemporary dictionaries use lofty language to define
this 1920s word: "a flippant gibe," says one; a "sardonic remark," claims
another. The whole *point* of a wisecrack is that it was usually off-the-cuff,
rude fare. Those highly skilled in this art were deemed "wisecrackers."

WISEGUY

A smart aleck (see page 184). A favorite term of Larry, Curly, and Moe in old Three Stooges movies—usually uttered just as one of them is about to crack another with a hammer or toss him out a window. ("Oh, a wise guy, huh? *Slap!*")

WOMBLE-CROPPED

A state of wretchedness or humiliation: "The poor dear was absolutely womble-cropped after she threw up on the altar at her wedding!"

WORRYWART

A fussbudget (see page 77).

WORSE THINGS HAPPEN AT SEA

This meant-to-be soothing old phrase—meaning "Relax: worse things have happened"—is at once perspective-giving and disturbing. After all, it compels you to imagine the mysterious awfulnesses that might have happened out there on all of those ships and schooners. But the end result is likely a positive one: once your mind has conjured up those unspeakable happenings, the problem that was worrying you in the first place will likely seem rather small and civilized by comparison. Also common once: the expression "Stranger things happen at sea."

XANTIPPE

In real life, she was Socrates' wife. Xantippe must have been quite a virago (see page 207), for her name later came to personify a "shrewish, scolding wife," according to *Grose's Classical Dictionary of the Vulgar Tongue* (1823).

YALLER-BOYS

Nineteenth-century American slang for "yellow boys," which was in turn slang for "gold coins." "Yellow fever" was, by extension, "gold fever."

SEE ALSO "COLD HARD CASH: TERMS FOR 'MONEY' OVER THE CENTURIES," PAGE 131

YAP

A rather coarse word for "mouth," usually inserted in one of the following configurations: "Shut your dang __" or "Quit flapping your __ ." Surprisingly, it was omitted from *Grose's Classical Dictionary of the Vulgar Tongue* (1823), which otherwise specialized in cataloguing this sort of fare. Other equally boorish old synonyms: "trap," "cakehole," "piehole," "kisser," and "yip."

YARN

As in, a "good yarn." A tall tale. An outlandish fib of a story. Let's bring back both the telling of such tales and this archaic word for them. By the way, in the old days, you used to "pitch a yarn," not "tell" one.

YEA-AND-NEA

A dumbbell; dolt. The sort of person who can only respond to a question by replying "yes" or "no."

"IT'S DÉJÀ VU ALL OVER AGAIN"

The Timeless Sayings of Yogi Berra

Many witticisms have elitist connotations. However, baseball icon Yogi Berra—who quit school after the eighth grade—remains the king of mensch wit. In case you've forgotten any of his Yogiisms, here's a list of some of his hallowed utterances—which should be preserved as national treasures.

On why he no longer patronized a popular St. Louis restaurant:

"Nobody goes there anymore; it's too crowded."

"It ain't over 'til it's over."

"When you come to a fork in the road, take it."

"You can observe a lot by watching."

"The future ain't what it used to be."

"If the world were perfect, it wouldn't be."

YELLOW-BELLIED

I.e., "dastardly" (see page 52), "chicken-hearted" (see page 34), and "lily-livered" (see page 118). The term sounds like it would have been coined west of the ol' Mississippi, but it actually originated in England. While some are tempted to claim that the "yellowness" invoked refers to a sickly—i.e., weak—complexion, others disagree. Says etymologist Gary Martin: "It is just as likely that 'yellow-belly' didn't refer to a person's complexion and had no literal meaning, but was simply a piece of nonsense name-calling." Either way, very few villains in Hollywood's old Westerns escaped without being dubbed "yellow-bellied varmints" or something *en par*.

YOU CAN'T JUDGE A BOOK BY ITS COVER

Coming generations won't even know what a book *is*, thus rendering this apt old saying more arcane than ever. It should be preserved and passed along regardless.

ZAD

Corrupt; crooked—like the letter "Z" itself. Imagine this revisionist Nixon statement:

> "In all of my years of public life, I have never obstructed justice. I welcome this kind of examination. People have got to know whether or not their president's zad. Well, I'm not zad."

ZIFF

A young "hooligan" (see page 96).

ZOUNDS

A circa-1600 exclamation of indignation or surprise: "She blew through her trust fund *already*? Zounds!" Sometimes written as "'Swounds!'", the word was an abbreviation of "God's wounds!"

ZOWIE

Another zesty expression of wonderment, this time from the 1930s. Usually it was rather cornily prefaced with the word "wowie" to give it some extra *oomph*. But with the "wowie" or without, it sounds endearing.

SEE ALSO "'WELL, I NEVER': AMUSINGLY QUAINT REACTION PHRASES," PAGE 211

fig. 31: END OF THE LINE

The
End

ABOUT THE AUTHOR

Lesley M. M. Blume is the author of *Let's Bring Back* ("Whimsical ... comical ... delightful" –*The New Yorker*) and *Let's Bring Back: The Cocktails Edition* as well as numerous critically acclaimed children's novels. She is a journalist and author based in New York City, and has covered fashion, media, and culture for many prestigious publications, including *Vanity Fair*, *The Wall Street Journal,* and *Vogue*, among others. Learn more about her at *www.lesleymmblume.com*.